A Practical Manual of Meditation

Also by Massimo Scaligero

The Light (La Luce)
An Introduction to Creative Imagination (2001)

The Secrets of Space and Time (2013)

A Treatise on Living Thinking
A Path beyond Western Philosophy,
beyond Yoga, beyond Zen (2014)

a practical manual of meditation

MASSIMO SCALIGERO

Translated by Eric L. Bisbocci

Lindisfarne Books
2015

2015

Lindisfarne Books

An imprint of SteinerBooks / Anthroposophic Press, Inc.

610 Main Street, Great Barrington, MA 01230

www.steinerbooks.org

Copyright © 2015 by SteinerBooks/Anthroposophic Press, Inc. Translation copyright © 2015 by Eric L. Bisbocci from the Italian edition by Teseo, *Manuale Pratico della Meditazione* (Rome, 1973/2005). All rights reserved. No part of this book may be reproduced, stored in a retrieval system, or transmitted in any form or by any means, electronic, mechanical, photocopying, recording, or otherwise, without the written permission of Lindisfarne Books.

Book design: William Jens Jensen
Cover image: Lotus, detail (shutterstock.com)

Library of Congress Control Number 2015944272

ISBN: 978-1-58420-190-8 (Paperback)
ISBN: 978-1-58420-191-5 (eBook)

Contents

Translator's Note	7
Preface	9
The Esoteric Structure of the Human Being	13
Freedom	19
The Formative Power of the Concept	28
Concentration	31
Meditation	36
Profound Concentration	38
The Spiritual Practice of Feeling	41
Breathing	44
Mental Silence	47
After The Meditation	48
Pure Perceiving	52
The Power of Imagination	59
The Exercise of the Rose Cross	66
The Power of Distraction	68
Instincts	71
The Exercise of Memory	73
Calm	75
Rosicrucian Method	79

Soul Ataraxia	82
Prayer	86
The Solar Opus	89
The Higher "I"	94
The Power of the Cross	98
The Force of Eros	104
Sacred Love	116
Karma	121
Fraternity and Sociality	129
Spiritual Practice	135
Pedagogy	139
The Path of Initiation	143
Spiritual Healing	152
The Function of Suffering	156
Inner Crisis	158
Anguish	163
Tiredness	165
The Joy of Existing	168
Diet	171
Rules of Initiation	175
Bibliography and Further Reading	187

Translator's Note

Throughout this book, Massimo Scaligero uses particular adjectives as nouns (e.g., *mental, mineral, sensory, suprasensory,* etc.). Though they bear a degree of concreteness or specificity in Italian, such is not the case in English. And so, when it is appropriate, I have occasionally inserted the implied words that he leaves out, such as *sphere, realm,* or *world* to compliment such adjectives and not leave them "hanging."

Although this work is born purely out of Anthroposophy, Scaligero occasionally uses certain Eastern terms that may be unfamiliar to Western esotericists. Having been profoundly steeped in both Eastern and Western esotericism, Scaligero employs such terminology, in order to bridge Western—or more precisely, Anthroposophical—concepts with those of the East. In this way, readers who are familiar with Eastern paths can more readily gain a foothold to better understand his thinking. Likewise, students of Anthroposophy can benefit by fathoming the correspondences between some of his Anthroposophical concepts and those embodied in the terminology of the East.

The distant stillness of constellations and the anxiety of Earth's Light, stir the rhythm of the soul, toward your endless gift.

Preface

Many signs give rise to the theory that dogmatism is the evil of the present time. By way of a radical investigation, it can be acknowledged that the ancient dogmatism of revealed truth could possibly have incarnated today in the form of a rigorous rationality that is hardly identifiable—the dogmatism of dialectics and science.

Endowed with semblances of progress, dogmatism can be recognized by the fact that each doctrine claims to proceed from its own object as if from an original fact, which is nonetheless conceived by means of an inner act that determines its basic value, but which, as such, eludes the subject involved in the research. For this reason, the object becomes the foundation, without really being it. In the intuition from which it moves, the subject does not recognize itself as a collaborative member of the foundation. As investigators or theorists, we identify our own "past thought" with the object; but this goes unnoticed. For this reason, the object arises before us as an entity founded upon itself. Rising to an original fact, sufficient unto itself, the object becomes an unconscious idol—accepted, in reality, according to a subtle faith. The unconscious faith is further developed in relation to the phenomenology that ensues from it—idolatry truly rises again in a scientific-technological form.

The subsequent inductive-deductive process is the dogmatic edifice that is logical, dialectical, and rigorous. But it is erected on a mystical foundation. The presupposition—as an inner act, which, possessed, could guarantee the development of the cognitive process according to reality—escapes conscious thought. Therefore, the object in its alterity excludes the human being. The dehumanization of culture has no other explanation.

The datum of science or dialectics acquires universal value outside the thinking that has validated it. Details illegitimately assume a universal role. It is the dogmatism that today pits one opinion against another, one human being against another, dialectic against dialectic, trend against trend, nation against nation—according to an incommunicability in which the logical-deductive relation substitutes the original relation that has been eliminated. The obtuse condition of thought nonetheless goes unnoticed, thanks to the perfect mechanism of the dialectic that moves it and that gives it the illusion of moving on its own. For this reason, it does not grasp anything of reality except what is thinkable and measurable—its most impoverished aspect, which presumes to be the whole of reality.

The remedy for this situation—which today is the foundation of a collective mental alteration unobserved by most, but surfaces as the common human neurosis, as the mystical persuasion of dialectical solubility of the questions truly impenetrable to dialectical thought, and as the incurable polemics between individuals, between factions—is the conscious restitution of the dynamic element of thinking, namely, a modern path to meditation. It is the reason for this manual, whose practical content springs from the experience of Western spiritual science, which includes, within itself, the ultimate essence of oriental techniques.

Those who believe they recognize, within this manual, the contradiction between the assumption of the conscious experience of meditation and the esoteric references that it uses for its elaboration, can be reassured by the very positivity of the method, which moves solely according to the logical mediations gradually required by the experience, up to that original immediacy of thought, which is the only one not in need of mediation—the true logic, the logic of the Logos. Only from such logic can the liberation of the human soul spring.

Technological civilization does not condition us, as some neo-Hegelians have with glib plausibility belatedly concluded. On the contrary, we do not manage to grasp the thinking from which such a civilization is born. The conditioning is not outside us in civilization, in society, or in the technological structure, but rather within us—within our thought, which lacks the inner dimension that allows it to arise as thinking. For this reason, we erroneously think the world devoid of such a dimension and, as such, we erect it, we deify it; we render it dominant in its legitimate logical dialectical form.

M. S.

The Esoteric Structure of the Human Being

We can recognize the human being as a synthesis of nature's kingdoms, ruled by the very principle that can be intuited at their origin. The univocal principle (which can be logically intuited at the foundation of nature) partially incarnates in us, and surfaces as the "I."

Such kingdoms are practically recognizable in the human constitution. They are: the mineral kingdom, which forms our visible physical body, referred to in Hinduism as *sthula sharira*; the structuring force of the plant kingdom, which forms our vital (or *etheric*) body, *linga sharira*; and the soul life of the animal kingdom, which operates in us as the sentient body, or *astral* body—*kama rupa*—by means of which we have a sensorial and sensual relation with physical life, not unlike that of the animal.

Added to this threefold constitution, of which the structural identity with the threefold domain of nature is recognizable, is a principle in the human being not found in the other kingdoms of nature, because it governs them from a higher level. It is the principle of individual consciousness, *atman*, or "I," itself essentially suprasensory, which imprints the correlation of the three systems up to "its corporeal appearing." It thus differentiates the human kingdom from the other kingdoms. The "I" that we normally speak of when referring to ourselves, is indeed *atman*, but this barely surfaces in our astral-etheric-physical organization. The vital-animal element is only partially ruled by that of the mental-spiritual.

Of the four constitutive human principles, only the mineral one is visible. The others operate imperceptibly. The etheric body is extra-spatial; the astral body is extra-spatial and extra-temporal; the "I" can be conceived as the void of that same astral body. One can also say that the physical body is a body woven of space; the etheric body is a body woven of time; the astral body is a body of extra-spatial and extratemporal light; the "I" is the essence of the light, insofar as it is identical to the light's principle. One can say that the "I"-astral-etheric-physical, or the spirit–soul–body relationship constitutes a hierarchy within itself.

All that the human being expresses on the physical plane, presupposes the dynamic of the three imperceptible principles. The action of these principles is perceptible in bodily form, which the presence of the "I" brings to a refinement lacked by the animal. It can nonetheless be deduced from the manifested activities of the soul, of thought, of self-consciousness. The damage of the psychic and physical life that leads us to illness, aging and death, originates in the alteration of the hierarchical relation of its principles with respect to their suprasensory essence. One can say that the sense of human life is the reconstitution of this relationship—the healing of the damage.

As human beings, we have the visible mineral body in common with the physical world, the invisible etheric body in common with the plant word, and the astral body—also invisible—in common with the animal world. By means of these, however, we operate as spiritual beings, becoming self-conscious thanks to a common inner activity that is our own, which, by means of the sense organs, reaches right down into the physical world. Under the first three aspects, we are related to the animal, which by way of the senses is moved by instincts and emotional impulses, since it depends on these without the possibility of autonomy. We, instead, transform our own sensations into thoughts at the corporeal, organizational level. We have the possibility of connecting to the spiritual principle what, on the animal plane, normally utilizes the spiritual according to an opposition to the spirit. We can control instincts and passions.

The spirit that manifests in the mineral as material fixity, in the plant as form, and in the animal as psyche, rises up in the human being as thought. At the level of thought, however, it lacks the power that is expressed as an imprint in the crystal, as form in the plant, as instinctive psyche in the animal. Nonetheless, it attains a self-identity—though initially reflective—in which it begins to express itself directly as the "I." The task of thinking is to realize, at its own level, the identity with itself, which the spirit renounces at the levels of Nature, in order to express itself as a psychic, vital and mineral structure.

Our inner *opus* is to realize the mediation that initially appears to us as thought. Thanks to this, we can reestablish the hierarchical correlation of the principles that we bear, that is to say, the "I," as *atman* must manage to govern the astral body and, through this, the etheric body and the physical body. When we will have spiritualized the astral and restored the original power to the etheric body, we will have transformed the physical body into a limb of the spirit, whose minerality will have the creative transparency, which for now, we can experience extraordinarily in pure thinking.

For now, the light of the "I" begins to light up only in thinking. When this light lights up, the life of feeling and the current of the will barely rediscover the original correlation. Such a possibility, however, resulting from the correct inner discipline, is rarely realized in us. The astral body normally binds us below to physical nature in the same way it binds the animal. Meanwhile, above, the light of the "I" permeates the astral body by means of reason. The astral body's nature therefore appears double—animal and spiritual. In ordinary human beings, these two natures are not separate. Rather, they are mixed up, and this mixture generates the continual contradiction of the soul's life. The unconscious prevalence of animal nature generates an ephemeral culture, false ideologies, erroneous orientations of science, perpetually unsatisfied passions, egoism, neurosis, and the series of illnesses.

The triumph of our lower nature over reason arises from the astral body's profound bond to the functions of nature. Such a bond ascends as a longing for life, regularly idealized and codified. Longing generates the inferior life of the "I," or egoism. Egoism generates aversion, an individual's regular opposition to other individuals—the daily human error, which of necessity becomes corrected by pain, sickness and finally death, if it is not dealt with by the spiritual principle that surfaces in the consciousness soul capable of controlling our lower nature by means of reason.

Because of its dual animal-spiritual nature, the astral body simultaneously bears within itself the impulses of sympathy and of antipathy, of attraction and repulsion, of pleasure and of pain, with respect to which, the possibility of distinction, of control and of conscious choice, belongs to the spiritual principle that surfaces as the "I." The impulses of animal nature and those of spiritual nature are mixed up within the astral body. For this reason, the soul continually oscillates confusingly between pleasure and pain, attraction and repulsion, if the "I" does not affirm itself as the principle of distinction and responsibility.

In the oscillation between the two opposites, as well as in their mix, the "I" is continually led to helplessly approve the soul's resulting *chaos*. This *chaos* is essentially an inversion of the hierarchy—spirit–soul–body—that we have already mentioned. The functions of the body involve the soul; the soul conditions the "I" by means of thinking, feeling and willing. As human beings, we are led to find, as true and just, what agrees with the instincts and that really imposes itself, ascending by means of willing and feeling from corporeal life. We believe that we choose by way of logical thought, according to the free "I." In reality, we give logical form to our choice according to the impulses of our animal nature.

Such an inversion of the spirit–soul–body relationship from which the series of human illnesses are derived—none excluded—has a single conscious remedy, namely, the discipline of concentration. The simple concentration exercise suggested in this treatise, according to rules drawn from direct suprasensory experience, that is, from the type of preparatory spiritual practice belonging to the Initiation of the new times, and not from texts prescribed by traditional Wisdom—from a technical point of view extraneous to the present human situation—restores the hierarchy, spirit–soul–body, even if for a brief moment. This moment, however, through our insistence on the discipline, can be prolonged and repeated with time.

The exercise must be extremely simple, due to the technique to which it conforms and the very aims of its execution. As we shall see, it consists of concentrating thought on an object that is devoid of special meaning. The physical object that we evoke and place at the center of our conscious attention, gives the "I" a way of operating—by means of thought—upon the forces of the astral body and, consequently, by means of these, upon the etheric-physical body.

In the simple concentration exercise, the spirit-soul-physical hierarchy— normally always altered—is temporarily restored. Therefore, it is the exercise that is least welcomed by our instinctive nature. It is also the most tiring despite its simplicity, and despite being the least fascinating. Sensational yogic or mystical exercises that appeal to our sentimental, or instinctive (animal) nature appear more convincing.

When we comprehend the wise use of concentration for restoring the intuited hierarchy, other types of exercises will gradually need to give the resurgent correlation (spirit–soul–body) a way to connect with the intentions of the human Archetype, so that our lower nature does not take advantage of it in a more subtle form. This lower nature tends to take on a spiritual vestment, and to use the spirit's initial powers for purposes that escape a rising self-consciousness. This is the present danger of irregular paths to the suprasensory.

All paths, for the fact that they exist, correlate to levels of the soul's development. But with respect to the evolutionary impulse of the present day, they can be recognized as irregular to the degree in which they ignore the process of thinking by means of which the spirit rises directly in the soul—according to a movement that is the inverse of the "traditional" one, where the soul once avoided thought in order to connect with the spirit, essentially escaping the human being.

Freedom

The freedom to which we aspire—giving it different meanings according to the level of our own development—is really (and solely) an event of thinking. Those who take away the freedom of others essentially have the power of giving substance to their own unfree thought. With such thought, they act as if they were free—ideologically and ethically convinced of their own prerogative.

Freedom is thinking that actualizes its own true nature, normally altered in the dialectical process. Dialectical thought can be free only on the dialectical plane. But, spiritually, such freedom is nothing. Thinking is free when it discovers its connection with the "I." This connection never really manifests, because dialectical thought is reflected, and in being reflected it does not have a connection with the "I" but, rather, with its psychic projection, the rational-sentient "I," the *ego*, the reflection of the "I."

In order for thinking to realize its true nature, it must experience its own free being; it is the soul's greatest experience. Thinking, in fact, normally manifests as the mediator of all sensory or extra-sensory knowledge—but never of itself. It is able to perceive itself only if, by means of concentration, it becomes isolated, even temporarily, from the psyche, from instincts, from sentiments, from sensory contents, from its own intellectual expression and from every content that is not its own pure being. In this pure being, it actualizes its own real nature. It becomes living. It expresses its own essential force as content—independent of the mechanism of dialectical intelligence. By means of such content, it can really encounter the sensory world, bearing to it the inner being that it lacks in appearing. It can, as a vehicle of the essence, simultaneously penetrate the soul.

Will and freedom proceed at an even pace in the discipline. The elevation and creative intensity of feeling, spring from thinking's agreement with the will. The training of the will corresponds to the liberation of thinking. The harmony of the three forces is the path of reintegration of the soul's light of life, capable of modeling physical corporeality—the ultimate sense of human earthly experience.

The question of freedom regards only thinking, insofar as such thinking loses its own real nature, by depending on the sphere of feelings and of the psyche through a dependence on the cerebral organ—by means of which it nonetheless becomes conscious at the sensory level. Such dependence is a state of thought's alienation, from which dialectics is born, as well as the logical-quantitative interpretation of the world and the series of ideologies that assume reality reflectively, outside the foundation.

Thought's dependence on the cerebral organ is contingent and temporary. It serves only, at a given phase of human evolution, to render thought independent of ancient spiritual authority, so that it can gradually realize such authority in the depths of its own autonomous movement. It is the instrumental dependence that gave rise to the quantitative knowledge of reality, beyond the qualitative one—which corresponds to the etheric, astral and spiritual sphere. In this way, it can isolate the sensory-quantitative world from its metaphysical foundation. The error of modern human beings is to assume the alienation of thought as normal, and to consider as real the quantitative vision that results from it. Meanwhile, the age of the exclusive experience of "quantity" is exhausted, having already given to thought what this thought expected from it—the logical possibility of freedom. The evil of present-day thought is its lack of consciousness with regards to what it has truly willed by means of scientific and technological experience.

By depending on the cerebral organ, and therefore on the sensory sphere, thought obligates feelings, willful impulses and the soul's aspirations to resound according to its alienation. Codified longing, the cult of animality, the negation of the spiritual, correlative instincts and passions, are born by rendering the state of deterioration absolute with regards to the function of thinking. It is the real alienation of the human being.

The question of freedom regards precisely the inner element by means of which the soul binds itself to the cerebral organ, in order to attain the logical knowledge of the sensory realm. The bond consists in the sensory dimension's irreversibility, that is, an illegitimate irreversibility, for it is due to thought's impotence to retrace its own movement. Meanwhile, its real task is precisely this—to retrace it. The question of freedom, therefore, regards thinking exclusively—not feeling, nor willing. The altered function of feeling and willing hinges on thought's lack of freedom, or better yet, on the psychic life's series of contradictions.

Our freedom depends upon freeing thought; there is no other freedom. Through the discipline of concentration, thought frees itself from the sensory element, from the resounding of the astral, and from the resounding of the etheric. It frees itself from the mechanism of logical structures, to the extent that it moves according to its own pure logic. It becomes the vehicle of the "I" within us. We rise up from our alienation. The action of free thought becomes liberating, when, through a harmony with the cosmic powers that support us, it manages to operate all the way to the etheric body.

The spiritual practitioner acts upon the etheric body by means of the will, that is, by operating on it by means of freed thinking. The direct action of freed thinking upon the etheric body is only stimulatory. Instead, only the cosmic-transcendent powers evoked by the ritual of liberated thinking can perform the transforming action. The thinking of concentration, meditating, and the pure idea are, in reality, acts of the "I," which appeals to such powers even if it does not imagine their existence.

To succeed in acting ritually upon the etheric body means to proceed toward the ultimate sense of liberation—Initiation. It means to overcome nature, the bonds of race, of family, of the collective animal entity. Furthermore, it means to begin weaving the true relationship with beings according to inner reality—the effective fraternity. This effective fraternity cannot be the correlation established on the basis of psychic-physiological necessity. The real fraternity is, per se, sufficient to resolve even problems inherent to such necessity.

Our lower nature possesses us through the etheric body's animal and instinctive memory, which is associative, as it is in the animal. The association escapes the light of the "I." It functions as automatism, normally attaining the powerless consent of the "I." The etheric association taken from the "I" is the basis of psychic illnesses—a phenomenon cultivated today by the analytical sciences of the psyche, as well as by spiritualism and the facile systems of yoga propagated in the world, with concentration techniques of the mediumistic kind.

Freedom, as a restitution of thought's original nature, is the liberation of higher (or spiritual) memory from lower (or animal) memory, namely, the deposit of the impulses of species, family, blood, etc. Lower memory normally controls us, making thought and its associative capacity its own. Real memory, on the contrary, contains the memory of our history all the way to that of preceding incarnations. Such memory, in the alienated human being, is in a state of sleep. It surfaces weakened in the psyche as instinctive memory, which expresses itself by means of the cerebral organ—at whose level it forms according to the system of rational knowledge.

Our animal memory uses the forces of spiritual memory, by means of thought's contingent dependence on cerebralism. Spiritual Science shows how the human brain is the organ that the spirit modeled ages ago in order to be able, by means of it, to act as the "I" upon physical nature. Initially, thought becomes autonomous from ancient metaphysical nature, by gradually binding itself to the cerebral instrument. From the need to determine itself by means of this instrument, it aspires toward freedom.

That which is animal in us affirms itself through cerebralism, namely, through the organ by way of which we think. Solar spiritual practice inverts such a process. It realizes thought's independence from cerebralism and establishes a rectifying relationship with the instinctive element. It is a reintegrating action, sometimes dramatically contrasted, by means of which the "I" recaptures its own primordial powers bound to physicality. Such a struggle takes place within consciousness, thanks to the forces of thinking that are gradually liberated, and thus, to the forces of memory, in a zone where lower nature and higher nature meet. Memory is not bound to cerebralism. Its forces—essentially suprasensory—are, nevertheless, normally used by what ascends into the mental sphere, as an instinctive current, by means of alienated thought, that is, thought conditioned by cerebralism: whereby there occurs an inversion of memory's real function, which tends to become constitutional.

According to the datum of recent experiments, the fact that memory can be stimulated by introducing a needle into the brain, does not mean that the brain contains memory, but that the brain's etheric body has been mechanically stimulated, just as perception stimulates it through the sense organs. By means of the needle, the perception of the ether is direct, but extraneous to the "I," insofar as it is provoked without the mediation of the organs of perception, whose content—when the "I" is not present—is usually connected with sentient memory through cerebral channels, sparking an association that gives rise to an instinctive response (as far as the well-known phenomenology of "conditioned reflexes"), in which the consent of the "I" is passive. The "I" does not grasp the concrete content of perception but, rather, what is suggested by associative memory, which is the association of memories on the astral-etheric plane, according to a mechanism characteristic of animal nature. In such a case, the etheric body's connectivity—even though it is an extra-sensory process—escapes the "I." It functions as automatism.

It is the path by means of which memories normally disturb weak-minded human beings, or invade them to the point of obsession. The sentient body evades the "I" by nevertheless using its force, which normally operates within consciousness with centripetal power. Such centripetal power essentially is overturned and therefore, acts against its principle. Each drug, each hallucination, each alcohol-based inebriation, each mediumistic yielding, each simplistic *yoga* with a combination of emphatic *mantras*, appeases an automatic power of concentration adverse to the "I," by preparing breakdowns of the soul and the body. The remedy for such a situation is, above all, one that is volitive-physical—the removal of causes and the recourse to a detoxifying therapy. But the radical cure is the capacity of the "I" to reestablish the force's flow, by means of the correct concentration, that is, through the legitimate use of the centripetal force, whose ultimate sense is the liberation of thinking—by means of which only the "I" can operate on the psychosomatic animal nature, rediscovering within the depths the powers of which this animal nature is the degradation.

Freedom is the ultimate sense of disciplines. True liberation is not the unchaining of oneself, which is always the explosion of physical nature—with its ideological codifications—but, rather, the chaining of oneself. To compel oneself according to an ironclad program, when it is an act of free thinking—i.e., free of human goals and, therefore, of longings, restores the original light to the etheric body.

Thinking is free in itself, but the etheric body, bound to animal nature, does not obey it. Therefore, thought is normally devoid of life. The more the etheric body is constrained by a rigorous discipline to elude its agreement with the longing inherent in the functions of nature, the more it becomes a limb of the spirit—an instrument of liberation. The path of freedom is to compel oneself; to command oneself; to follow the most difficult path; to endure in a positive way all that is heavy and which conditions. The more our animal nature is led to obey and to respond to a rhythm that governs it, the more it again becomes the power of the higher principle of the "I," and, therefore, the cooperator of the human being's reintegration.

If we have well understood the sense of what is here called constriction, as the spiritual practice of the etheric body, it will not be difficult to understand that such a constricting is not a forcing, or a coercing, but an inner mediating that is absolutely free, namely, an acting by way of conscious mental images upon the current of the will, giving it tasks from which the etheric body—through its habitual agreement with animal nature—tends to escape.

No creation or human loftiness exists that does not call for a long sacrificial effort of liberation from the inertia of the psycho-physiological nature. In this direction, we can recognize the mission of thought. In reality, the conscious human being tears the formative virtue of the concept from the etheric body's noblest forces, allowing their power of metaphysical synthesis to resound within the physical sphere, as the structure of knowledge.

The Formative Power of the Concept

What spiritual practitioners really tend to experience, by means of disciplines, is the force by means of which the concept forms in consciousness. No concept manifests without such a formative power, but this normally remains ignored, since the ordinary rationalist is interested only in the dialectical use of the conceptual form. Instead, as spiritual practitioners, we take on the concept as a vehicle of the power of thinking. We go back to the formative power of the concept, independent of its specific meaning. Each concept presupposes such a power, insofar as it is the synthesis of a multiplicity that corresponds to a real entity as an original extra-sensory "type."

As present-day dialecticians, we normally ignore the moment of synthesis. While we assume its power to be real, we effectively do not even believe in its existence. We fail to notice that, with the concept of "horse," we refer to a single entity that lives in all horses and indicate it as something concrete. We do not know what we even do. We believe a "universal" to be real, whose existence we dialectically negate or ignore. Without knowing it, we tap the concept's formative power, or power of life. By means of concentration, we, as disciples, experience precisely the life element of which thought is normally deprived. In reality, no concept of modern dialectics bears its own content as life. An ideology's series of concepts is regularly a system of the non-knowledge of inner life, to which it nevertheless refers (see the concepts of fraternity, morality, value, universality, etc.) No advocate of fraternity believes that there exists, as a fraternity, a univocal, non-physical force, operating in a concrete way precisely by virtue of its non-physical being.

The concentration exercise restores realism to concepts. In effect, when we evoke a concept, we solicit a force that enables it to surface, but it immediately withdraws into the unknown of consciousness. It is the force of memory, which manifests in the thinking movement and immediately yields to the abstract-dialectical form at which level it becomes conscious. A concept remembered is an act of creation forever new, but the living moment of the mnemonic act continually escapes dialectical consciousness, to the extent that such consciousness is bound to cerebralism. The living moment of the concept or of its memory, being preconscious, is instead unbound to cerebralism. Concentration appeals to this living moment: thanks to it, thinking reaches its own foundation, which is not the cerebral organ. Such a foundation is a primordial force of the soul, which tends to rise again aware. Those who will someday confront human problems according to reality, that is, according to a meditative penetration, rather than an ideology, will need to be capable of reawakening such a force.

The force that enables the concept to surface in the mind when evoked is the same force at work in the original formation of the concept. In both cases, this force springs as a power, within an inner zone that escapes consciousness. In concentration, consciousness tends to make this power its own, which its movement continually presupposes.

We can therefore evoke a concept, because essentially we already possess it. We possess an indefinite series of concepts of things and entities, but, if we observe, never have we effectively operated with deliberate forces of consciousness in their formation. A higher force, in the form of a greater spontaneity, has acted in the thinking relationship with the object.

We consciously only have mental pictures of an entity. We end up having a concept of it, which, in itself, is a power of synthesis, but we have not directly worked upon such a synthesis through an act of determined consciousness. Nevertheless, we normally use the concept as if we possessed such a synthesis. It is as if by saying "horse" we have the perception of the entity that lives in each single horse, as its archetype. Concentration consists in consciously acquiring the dynamics of the archetypal process, which surfaces in the conscious mental sphere from the depths of the soul.

If we can experience the concept's power of synthesis, we enter a sphere of reality that is normally imperceptible, because it is vast and powerful for the conscious mental sphere. We enter a sphere of suprasensory powers, which we perceive as the absolute foundation of the sensory sphere. As free beings, we today have the power of proving to ourselves the reality of the suprasensory world.

The preconscious activity by means of which the concept is formed can be experienced as the primordial inner current that transforms matter into spiritual energy in the organism, and spiritual energy into living nature. In this activity, the present-day spiritual practitioner has the possibility of gathering what tantric Yoga calls *Shakti*, in particular, the current of *kundalini*. It is the power that is unattainable by means of such Yoga, because it is impossible for its technique to be current.

Concentration on an object that we evoke essentially moves from its concept, that is, from its element that inside consciousness is a working power of synthesis, un-possessed. This power becomes objectified. The "I" lives with its own current of force within the soul, thanks to the fact that, through a series of mental pictures, the object is reconstituted as a concept, namely, as an original synthetic power.

So that it can allow itself to be perceived, this power, substantially woven of will, demands the insistence of the will in thinking. It becomes willed to such an extent that thought's determination and its willful content end up coinciding. The will is willed so intensely that it ceases to demand effort. It becomes a current of life that reconnects consciousness to the source of its force.

Concentration

Concentration is the key exercise of the discipline, and therefore, the vehicle of illumination and of freedom. It consists in gathering, by means of a theme, the flow of thinking in a single point, in order to attain a dynamic synthesis. This synthesis objectively realizes what thought is originally.

Thought is originally a power of synthesis, but at such a level it does not know its own content, because it is not conscious of itself. Normally, thinking becomes conscious of itself by turning to the sensory, by assuming the sensory as its own content or its speculative echo. In consciousness directed toward the sensory, thinking immediately becomes analytical and dialectical, but opposed to its own original nature. Concentration restores to thought this original nature, which the spiritual practitioner recognizes to be one with the universal forces that support its existence.

The operation consists in reconstituting, from an object or from a theme, the thinking synthesis at its foundation, by retracing its dialectical-analytical development, until discovering its initial pure concept. The conceptual determination, however, can be completely grasped to the extent that it is an evocation of a human-made product. From such an object, the spiritual practitioner can extract all the analytical thought by means of which the object was constructed—reascending this thought until recovering it as the intuitive thinking that conceived the object, namely, (until recovering it) as the concept.

The object is to be simply evoked, not simultaneously perceived. To perceive it during the exercise would be a mistake, since the task is to experience thinking free of sensory supports. In reality, the idea of a human-made object lies not in the object, but in the human mental realm. Meanwhile, the object that belongs to living nature (crystal, plant, animal, etc.) immanently bears, within itself, its own idea. Here, the idea is present as the power of its form. The correlation of a crystal's parts is inherent in the form-type of its system of crystallization, whereas the correlation of a machine's parts is organically devoid of meaning, corresponding to an abstraction of the human mental realm, extraneous to the real relationship of the mineral substantiality of a "piece" with that of other "pieces."

From mental picture to mental picture, the exercise mnemonically reconstitutes original synthetic thinking. Therefore, the object cannot be anything that is not produced by human beings. It cannot be a crystal, or a plant, or an animal, or the sky, etc. Concentration on these objects does not realize the wisdom of the exercise, which consists in drawing from an object all the thinking that thought it, so as to be able to eliminate the sensory support and be in the presence of the synthesis-idea. In the crystal, in the plant, in the sky, etc., we find ourselves before an object that incarnates a thought that is not our thought, and that we can therefore only speculatively grasp as a conceptual determination. But the concentration exercise has nothing to do with speculative processes, which sometimes, instead, can be called to cooperate, according to a conscious dosage, in the exercise of meditation.

We indeed connect ourselves, through our thinking, with objects that express the "universe" thinking that operates as living nature, but thanks to another type of exercise that demands the perception of the object. The perceptive contemplation of the object and that of the non-human thinking that incarnates within it, constitute a single soul movement. They, however, reenter another moment of the discipline. They are not the typical concentration exercise, the key to liberating the thinking with which we think daily, and of which the present paragraph concerns itself.

As spiritual practitioners, we must proceed from the thinking with which we ordinarily think. We must free this thinking. For this reason, we must begin with objects that typically express our present rational, dialectical thinking. From this, we can arrive at our own thinking activity independent of the object. Such a freed activity manifests to us as the first conscious experience of the spiritual.

If we were to begin concentrating on objects in which universal thinking is directly expressed, we would never arrive at it, because we would, nonetheless, always move by means of our own mental picturing bound to the sensory realm. We would mediate the universal abstractly with a thought that nevertheless bears within itself an opposition to the Universal. This observation can be extended to each exercise that we deem to be valid thanks to its immediate regularity with respect to the suprasensory, but which essentially impedes the conquest of immediate thinking, that is, of the liberating mediation.

The concentration exercise consists in evoking a human-made object that, preferably, is exhaustible in a minimal series of mental pictures, by means of which the maximum thinking-force can be expressed. Therefore, it must be the simplest of objects.

Since the goal of concentration is to experience the synthetic element of thinking, normally alienated in the analytical-rational process, the object must be one whose meaning does not exert any influence upon the operation, since this operation demands only the arid a-psychic willful determination of thought. The original force of thinking lies within this willful determination. We only need to discover it. This force is itself in movement within the activity aimed at discovering it. Such movement is fundamental to the whole life of the soul and its relation with the spirit and the body, because, for the first time, the typical order, "I"-soul-body, normally contradicted by everyday experience is realized. Therefore, this basic exercise is the key to the equilibrium and wellbeing of the soul and the body. The fact that—despite its elementary nature—it is always difficult to realize, can be explained by means of its truly exceptional task, namely, to be the ideal operation that reconstitutes the original equilibrium of the formative human principles.

The wisdom of the exercise lies in its simplicity. One evokes the object—needle, or pencil, or button, etc.—and describes it with precision. One then briefly makes out its history and individualizes its function. This essential operation, conducted with a least amount of indispensable mental pictures, finally gives rise to an image synthesis, or concept, which is useful to keep before one's consciousness, objectively, as the initial image of the object. The more such an image-synthesis can be objectively contemplated, the more the concentration becomes the experience of the spirit. During the exercise, one must not be distracted by any other thoughts. If this distraction occurs, one must reascend the unrelated mental image to the point in which it illegitimately intervened.

Meditation

Meditation distinguishes itself from concentration for the fact that, while concentration takes up an object, or a theme—independently of its meaning—as a means for the dynamic synthesis of thinking, "meditating" is thinking that moves directly according to the spiritual meaning of an object or a theme. In concentration, the content of thinking is of no importance. Rather, one makes sure that it is unrelated to the interests of the spirit. In meditation, however, the content, insofar as it is spiritual, arouses in its pure immediacy the movement of thinking, namely, the imagining, which simultaneously connects feeling and willing to thinking.

One turns to a content that can be immediately had as an image. Such an image must correspond to an inner objective experience. Therefore, it must be drawn from a text of Spiritual Science or one of traditional wisdom, or else suggested by a spiritual instructor. For example, "Terrestrial gold is the mineral trace of the Sun." It is not a matter of analyzing the concept of "gold" or of "Sun," nor of rationally analyzing the relationship between them but, rather, of assuming the image as it directly manifests in the words, that is, of receiving the immediate resounding of these words within the soul. The three forces of the soul—thinking, feeling, and willing—in their pure state, are simultaneously recalled in this immediate resounding.

To meditate is to nourish, contemplatively, the element of life by which the image initially arises in consciousness. Meditation does not demand any reflection; like concentration, it, too, is essentially a simple operation. It is not to argue. It is not to analyze by means of thoughts, or to investigate in order to discover hidden meanings but, rather, to contemplate by imagining or to imagine by contemplating the assumed content, until arriving at the calm perception of the image-synthesis or the feeling that corresponds to it. Nothing more. Since the image-synthesis and the corresponding feeling usually rise up immediately, there is no other task but to let them live within the soul. As soon as they die down, the art of the spiritual practitioner is to renew again its rising moment for a given number of minutes, so as to impregnate the soul with it. Such a technique is also valid for meditations that require the connection of different systems of images—like, for example, the Rosicrucian exercise—and are actualized by means of mental images that leave out sensory reality, as deliberately arbitrary constructions, united in the depths by a precise suprasensory content (see "The Power of Imagination").

In essence, to meditate is not to intuitively elaborate spiritual themes. This, if anything, is a cognitive operation later possible by means of forces drawn from meditating. Least of all, it is a dialectical or logical analysis. The exercise of the dialectical-logical intellect, in the majority of cases, is a preliminary training for the concentration exercise.

On the contrary, to meditate is to directly arouse the soul forces by means of a spiritual content. That which rises up spontaneously from its engagement, is received and nourished. Since the inner force matters more than its dialectics, the task of the spiritual practitioner that meditates is—when all is said and done—to render continuous and objective, for a certain number of minutes, the initial moment of the lighting up of inner forces according to a given theme of the spirit—namely, an image, a phrase or a symbol, which winds up being capable of resounding by way of its own force within the soul.

Profound Concentration

The object, theme, concept, or image, or sign of light, or symbol, that we, as pupils, attain as a final synthesis of concentration, must remain objectively before us. It is not important which form it clothes, or that it has any form. We should not care about seeing anything with a given form. Rather, we should care about seeing before us the *quid* that formally or informally symbolizes thinking-synthesis. This *quid* can also be a nothing, and nonetheless be there, as "a willed imperceptible."

This *quid* is to be contemplated calmly, with decisiveness, with utmost attention, with subtle continuity of will, that is, by simultaneously cultivating a spontaneous rest within oneself—a contemplative detachment, which realizes the power of profound inertia, or "Ataraxia" (see "Ataraxia of the Soul"), according to the intense incorporeal activity objectified by virtue of concentration. This intense incorporeal activity is essentially the original identity of the "I" with things, which is awakened, even for a brief moment.

As pupils, we understand the importance of contemplating the sign-symbol in a state of silent purity. Such purity is essentially the independence of the "I" from the soul. In fact, concentration is realized to the degree in which it is not altered by feelings, memories, tensions, psychicisms, and psychosomatic states. Like a mathematical formula—arid and objective, clear of psyche, and therefore, extra-subjective—the sign-symbol must remain before the experimenter, with its invisible light, which excludes any personal element of the soul.

True strength is to keep the sign of light outside oneself in its intact adamantine state, or in its absolute impersonality. It is the symbol of the liberation of the "I" within the soul—that is, the beginning of its autonomy from the astral body, or from the psychic field where it is the continuous circle of instincts and of emotional states.

Concentration is realized beyond what we constitutionally are, by means of an independence from the mental and physical condition to which we have identified ourselves.

Concentration must not operate by means of the forces of what we existentially are, but by means of the most liberated thinking. Essentially, it is added to what we are. The psychophysical being that we are must not intervene in the slightest. It must be temporarily ignored. Meanwhile, yogic or traditional methods involve its participation in the inner *opus*, or better yet, they use it. This distinction is important.

The stream of thinking attention, as an incorporeal force capable of acting beyond the body, and, therefore, on the body, must be developed to the utmost outside the organism to which it has become identified by way of the soul. It is to be activated beyond ourselves, outside the normal marasmus that we bear as psychosomatic life, regardless of tiredness, or illness, or depression, or exultation, or existential impossibility, or traumatic event. Indeed, precisely the psychosomatic impediment can facilitate the distinction from it of the activity that transcends it.

The object of concentration right down to its clear light must be simply perceived, beyond the feeling of the body or of the psyche. Feeling normally reconnects consciousness with corporeality and paralyzes the force. To realize the clear light (or extrasensory sign) of the object—which is truly extinct as a physical object—beyond what we are, means to overcome the suggestive-instinctive element of the psyche, which normally tends to make each inner operation its own—be it of Yoga, of Magic, or of Mysticism—through subtle feeling, tied to corporeality. In the self-feeling bound to the corporeal being, extrasensory forces adverse to our freedom normally control us. Concentration, by becoming operative, postulates therefore a spiritual practice of feeling.

The Spiritual Practice of Feeling

The spiritual practice of feeling is realized by any exercise that harmonizes thought with the will. Feeling is the extra-conscious force, which, in its essence, connects thought with the will. Ordinary feeling is not the real life of feeling but, rather, its alteration. Such an alteration is rectified by the exercise of the will's correspondence to freed thinking.

Feeling, as a pure soul force, can rise up, there, where normal feeling (which is nonetheless the vehicle of our animal nature) is silenced. As a result of meditation, feeling tends to rise up as the soul's force of rhythm, already in that sense indirectly urged by each prudent connection between thought and the will. In order for the power of the soul's rhythm to manifest directly, the state of absence of normal feeling must be technically produced—like a passage open to depersonalized feeling, capable of being immersed in the interests of others and the world, with the spontaneity that is normally aroused by personal interests.

In certain occasions, we must train ourselves to forbid the normal reaction of feeling. The exercise of "not feeling" is the condition for pure concentration and the consequent resurrection of feeling, that is to say, for the surfacing of pure feeling, which frees the mental sphere from corporeality. But, similarly, pure thinking opens the way to non-feeling and frees the mental sphere from sentient-rational subjectivity.

The power of attention directed to an object, suspends the nervous system's conditioning of the inner activity, but precisely this temporary immobility of the nervous system corresponds to the "void" of egoic feeling. The habitual nervous reaction ceases to govern the soul's life. The absence of astral tension that ensues from it becomes the area in which the flow of the pure thinking-force is possible. But one must simultaneously say that the awakening of the pure thinking-force makes the astral void possible—the area necessary for the surfacing of the cosmic principle of thinking.

The temporary absence of subjective feeling realizes consciousness' detachment from the nervous system, that is, the independence of the higher astral—wherein lives the "I"—from the lower astral in which the "I" is obtusely controlled. This detachment isolates the inner entity within the nervous system and reduces it to its legitimate function. This inner entity controls the life of instincts by means of such a system.

In reality, by virtue of non-feeling, we temporarily become independent of the collective entity that governs the blood; that is to say, we arrest the action of the entity, "Lucifer"—the inspirer of emotions, of passions, of moods, and of thoughts that contradict the soul's essence. However, by suspending the influence of the Adversary that acts within the blood, even for brief moments, we automatically isolate the Adversary that acts through the nervous system.

The Spiritual Practice of Feeling

We render the soul independent of the "ahrimanic" entity that totally expresses itself within the instinctive human being by controlling the nervous system. In such moments, the nervous system limits itself to being the pure transmitter, or the neutral mediator, according to the same process by which it operates in the sense organs. In effect, the sense organs function as objective mediators, because, in them, the action of the emotional (or instinctive) entity is excluded, having been originally eliminated by the edifying forces of the "I." The senses truly do not deceive. It is thought that does not manage to be, within itself, consciously alive with respect to them, like when it lights up with their content, thanks to the neutral mediation of the nervous element.

Even if temporary, the mental sphere's independence from the nervous system, restores the hierarchical correlation spirit–soul–body, by reawakening an original power of the spirit in relation to its own astral-ether-physical being.

Constitutionally the blood is the physical support of the "I"; the nervous system is the support of the astral; the glandular system is the support of the etheric body. During moments in which the lower feeling that expresses the alteration of the above-mentioned hierarchical relationship is suspended, the "I" flows in the blood according to its transmuting light. Therefore, it simultaneously tends to restore to the nervous system—rendered immobile—its original metaphysical life. In fact, as a result of a metaphysical original life lost by the nervous system, the ahrimanic entity can control it without conflicts, even if, within the sense organs, such control has the limit mentioned. In reality, through the vehicle of the nerves, the ahrimanic entity not only impedes the perception of the suprasensory—that supports the world everywhere—from reaching us, but, moreover, it manages to stamp its own influence onto the bloodstream, by rising to the head and penetrating the mental sphere with destructive impulses. The spiritual practice of suspending feeling establishes an interval whereby the relationship between the spiritual and the corporeal is reactivated—as it is during sleep—temporarily bringing a change to the type of breath and to its connection with the rhythm of the blood.

Breathing

Concentration realizes relationship between consciousness and the breath. Breathing is normally the rhythmic expression of the lower astral body's control within the organism. With the conditioning of the nervous system suspended and the "void" of feeling realized, the breath ceases to move according to the lower astral body. Gradually, it frees itself from the nervous system. But this does not have to be noticed, or followed, even if we know that it is occurring.

If the breath is gradually led to an essential autonomy, it reacquires the rhythm of the higher astral, which belongs to it in the depths, but from which it is normally alienated. Nonetheless, it is not a deliberate breathing discipline that can restore to the breath its secret light but, rather, the "ataraxia" (calm) of the rational-sentient astral—something that can be called a zero of psychic life, a metaphysical airiness, in which the forces of the foundation surface. Only at this stage can the adequate breathing exercise be practiced. In our other works, we were able to speak about a state of *"christic" ataraxia,* as a requirement for the new type of breathing.

We can lead breathing to a state of functional tranquility, from which, in reality, it is born, and perceive such tranquility as a state of absolute independence from the nervous system. It is a state that can be reached from a direction other than that of the nervous system, thanks to the mentioned discipline of "non-feeling." This corresponds to profound concentration, namely, to the perception of living thinking, outside of what we are as individuals who derive self-consciousness from the nervous system.

Breathing can become a vehicle of the pure extra-corporeal force, not insofar as we operate on it according to the techniques of *pranayama*—that today inevitably solicit the inner workings of the corporeal nature, where the spiritual is alienated—but insofar we perceive its pre-corporeal being, freed of the rational-sentient astral, and its "proceeding" from a cosmic rhythm, bound not to feeling but, rather, to willing, which is to say, to original feeling, to the constitutional purity of the corporeal being, independent of the nervous system. As one can see, it is a breathing that has little to do with that of Yoga techniques.

The breath is normally the support of feeling. But since this feeling is the psychic movement of subjectivity, it is the breath that expresses the subordination of the spiritual to corporeality, that is, the vital nourishment of the ego, of illness, of bodily destruction. We cannot operate ascetically by way of such breathing. It asks only one thing—to be left alone.

Becoming free of the nervous system allows breathing to be the vehicle of the light's metaphysical vitality. Such a possibility corresponds to that of the liberation of feeling, or of the extinction of subjective feeling, illegitimately inherent to the nervous system. The unbound breath develops as a rhythm of willing. It becomes a relation of depth with the power of the cosmic Entity that has the element of *air* as a support on Earth. Air is the sensory vehicle of the light.

In the same way that the inner human being has the mineral body as physical support, there exist on Earth suprasensory Entities whose earthly support is respectively constituted of elements such as fire, air, water etc. When we free the breath from the nervous system, pursuant to the freeing of thought from cerebralism and to the quiet of feeling, we perceive the metaphysical element of the breath. We begin to experience the Archangel of the Air—the function of whose action has been revealed to some pupils by the Master of the new times (Rudolf Steiner).

The secret of the Philosopher's Stone is linked to the knowledge of this breathing, granted by the spiritual world to the pupil who becomes incapable of making personal use of the force. Those of us who know this breathing, in reality, feel that we must minimally resort to it and that only in rare moments can we deserve to make use of its help, to the extent that the content of holiness born from it, necessarily encounters a profound inadequacy in the soul's current egoic state.

We become directly informed of the moment in which we can become conscious of the metaphysical breath, and of the radical rhythm that it requires in order to become again the vehicle of the light.

Mental Silence

The thinking of concentration, if possessed, can be brought to absolute quiet. It is not eliminated; instead, it is united with its essence. We unite with this essence, by gathering the powers of the soul around it—silently, preventing the soul from giving it any form. The thinking force becomes immobile, united, and identical to itself. It identifies with its own original silence. It generates mental silence.

Going forward in the discipline, we who believe that we have the maturity to gain access to a higher level of experience, must willingly eliminate the suprasensory contents received by means of mental silence, until attaining a more radical type of silence. This more radical silence is what e esoteric literature has customarily called the void. It is clear that, as pupils, we can turn to it, to the extent that the initial mental silence attained by virtue of concentration has become familiar to us.

All higher experiences are mediated by mental silence. Each further ascent of consciousness presupposes the possession of a level from which it moves and from which it is occultly related to every other level—lower or higher. Each ascent demands the possibility of eliminating, by means of the void, the suprasensory contents attained at the level from which it moves. Mental silence, in essence, readies the experience of the void. But the ascent to a level of higher consciousness continually demands to be mediated by the void of the suprasensory content possessed.

Mental silence constitutes a positive conquest by the experiencer. It is not only the peacemaker of the psyche and the nervous system, but, above all, it is the passage opened to the higher forces of the "I."

After The Meditation

After the meditation, the suprasensory force that is evoked tends to become life. Yet, in order to incarnate, it needs the operator's ordinary state of wakefulness, that is, the state of positive unconsciousness proper to the ordinary activity of the soul-physical organism. It demands that we forget the completed operation and immerse ourselves into everyday life with dedication. In the *spontaneity* of action, the evoked forces are led to flow to the extent that they go unseen. To see them or notice them is their paralysis. This positive forgetting, nonetheless, does not mean that we must forget the responsibility regarding ordinary life that we derive from meditation.

Just as the cosmic forces that restore our etheric-physical vitality can operate thanks to sleep, so, too, do the forces evoked in concentration and in meditation need that positive state of sleep of the soul-physical organism, which is its normal spontaneity during the waking life. It must be emphasized that the phenomenon of sleep regards only the human head, where a change of polarity of consciousness occurs. Meanwhile, the rest of the etheric-physical organism remains with the astral and the "I" in the identical relationship that it has in the waking state.

The difference consists in the fact that during the waking state, the "I" and the astral, lacking their cosmic connection, and therefore, their real wisdom, operate destructively upon the etheric-physical organism by means of the normal process of instincts and passions. During sleep, the "I" and the astral are, instead, in communion with their original state, according to a fullness not permitted during the waking state by what transforms experience into the content of consciousness, namely, the cerebral organ. Truly, in the head, we are ordinarily at the mercy of instincts and passions.

Elevating the "I" and the astral to their cosmic dominion during sleep, essentially equals a descent of the "I" into the medial center's transcendent system of forces (or the thorax) and more deeply, into that of the will center, which is also the center of the processes of metabolism and of the dynamisms of instinctiveness—centers from which the "I" must temporarily separate itself together with the higher astral, so that the experience of their transcendent systems of forces by way of sleep can be possible to it. Each insurgence of the lower astral against the higher, obstructs the detachment of this (higher astral) and, therefore, impedes or renders the process of sleep difficult.

To penetrate with the "I" into the suprasensory realm by virtue of solar spiritual practice, is essentially to descend into the depths of the corporeal organization. It is not a descent of the rational or mental "I" but, rather, of the pure "I." Therefore, at the end of the meditation, we give ourselves to ordinary life; we spontaneously immerse ourselves into action, since the evoked forces of the pure "I" that tend to penetrate the corporeal organization, descend according to their solar quality, or "their flowing from" the Logos—for which they need non-consciousness or the everyday condition of sleep of both the rhythmic life, as well as the volitive-instinctive one.

The inner operations occur on the stage of mental consciousness. But such consciousness must not follow them into the organic depths where they have arrived. These operations demand to be actualized, unseen. We must limit ourselves to operating by means of pure thinking and imaginative *dynamis*, independent of corporeality. Only in an advanced phase of development, can we act directly on the astral-etheric currents, but always by means of imaginative determination. The spiritual practice becomes a liberating descent into corporeality's profound systems of force.

One day, direct action will be possible to the degree in which the spirit has become nature, or instinct. As pupils, we are presently preparing this future possibility.

In certain moments, we notice the profound identity of the "I" with beings, things, and the world, as if a single "I" were at their center like a real fountain of fraternity, and we catch sight of how we essentially oppose this higher human unity with a series of ideological pretenses of ethicalness, progress and sociality.

For those of us capable of assuming responsibility for our own inner development, the moments of the original unity of the "I" with things and with beings, can be extended and repeated during the day. We will be able to proceed by understanding that development, as an end in itself—one conditioned by earthly aims or by previous representations of a spiritual activity to be carried out on Earth—makes no sense.

Only the suprasensory level that is attained can illuminate the type of action. But we can recognize the same pure action, the discipline and ascetic *opus* as what, by our own virtue, creatively operates within the Earth's suprasensory sphere. The consequences of human thinking, feeling, and willing are received by cosmic Entities that transform them into the current of destiny.

Inner individual action can reach such impersonality, so as to work for collective humanity. There is a current of karma that goes back centuries and millennia, but it expresses itself according to a form determined by the possible ritual action of spiritual communities, namely, of *élites* immune from ideologies.

The discipline of concentration ceases to be a subjective technique, when we receive the virtue of impersonality from the thinking that has been freed. Moving forward toward profound concentration, we understand the importance of reconnecting individual intelligence with cosmic intelligence, of which the former is the degradation. To strengthen thought is not enough. Thought must become conscious of the moral tenor that the attained level requires of it.

Individual intelligence, strengthened by means of concentration, can unconsciously reinforce the lower subjective limit, which opposes it to cosmic intelligence. We attain living solar thinking, only when we open up to the knowledge of the Entity that supports cosmic intelligence, the Archangel of Thinking. Our thinking becomes liberated from the mental-cerebral realm, which is to say, from the current of the *ego*. Then, it can know everything, without the mediation of books or doctrines, because in our very soul we see the secret of life unfolding. Our connection to this secret is the path of the Holy Grail. The Rosicrucian path—to the extent that it is the "direct path"—differentiates itself from every other present-day path, because of the need to connect the meditative current with the guidance of the Archangel of Thinking.

Pure Perceiving

It is the technique by means of which we, as pupils, manage to experience the inner process of sensory perception. We move from a given perception and direct our attention to it, which gradually gives us a way to have before us a content independent of the subjective form that normally clothes it. Essentially, we separate the mental image and feeling from this content.

In perceiving, we gather the presence of an unconscious inner life in the immediate form in which it ordinarily appears. Life's form and content are identical, for which the form is itself the content that we contemplate, but to the extent that we simultaneously separate this form from its sensory imprint. By means of the mentioned exercise, we begin to perceive the vital (or etheric) element.

By virtue of the attention deliberately turned toward a perception—just as we learned to turn it toward a thought in concentration—we practice isolating its suprasensory content. In concentration, we usually manage to contemplate our own past thought. In the exercise of pure perceiving, we contemplate a past thought that is more powerful, namely, that of creative nature. This thought can arise in us, to the extent that we bring a silent consciousness toward it. It is thought that we do not have to think; we simply allow it to act within the soul.

It makes no sense to contemplate a human-made object. Such an object can only be evoked through the concentration exercise. However, it cannot be contemplated through the exercise of pure perception, which requires objects, whose creating thought is immanent. Only the distinction between the perceptions of the inanimate human-made product and the animate product of nature can, in preparatory way, be useful to the aims of a comparison between the two types of perception. In an advanced phase of the spiritual practice, we can experience—by means of inner perception (which "spirit" inhabits the human-made inanimate object).

The perception of nature's living being is, however, mediated by the mineral element in which it appears and for which it is sensory. Through the purity of immediacy proper to perceiving, we realize, in earthly minerality, the support in which the "I" directly expresses itself with its power of identity. We can consciously realize this power of identity.

By encountering earthly minerality in ordinary perceiving, the "I" resurrects from this—as the life of consciousness—the inverted spiritual powers that sleep. But consciousness is normally closed to this "inner resurrecting" of minerality's transcendent reality from perception, because it is engrossed in the subjective appearing of forms, which are alive, but rise up as forms of a death process—a process that moves from us, identifying (at that level) with a degree of nature's death. That reality is nonetheless at the point of resurrecting in the "appearing" mediated by perception. But we obtusely flee from it, binding ourselves by way of longings to the immediate sensory image of reality, namely, to the form grasped by the sentient soul, which is the vestment of minerality's state of death. This minerality, instead, is on the verge of resurrecting by means of color, sound, taste, fragrance, etc.—the qualitative immeasurable, which surfaces in perception.

In truth, perception does not manifest in order to be enjoyed as sensation, but in order to be experienced as the power of the "I," which springs from its encounter with physical minerality. The "I" is truly on the verge of allowing metaphysical reality to live of physical minerality, by defeating the power of enchantment for which the appearing of minerality, which imprints feeling and sentient willing with itself, rises to physical reality—no differently than a powerful hallucination. Such hallucination is nourished by desire.

In ordinary perception, a magical transmuting act—continually lost in favor of the longing for the apparent sensory content—is to be gathered. It is a direct relation of the "I," of a power with respect to which waking consciousness is inadequate, like a catalectic state of consciousness with respect to the waking state. It can be said that the art of Solar Magic consists in conquering—as the power of waking consciousness—what the "I" already realizes by having the world rise up in perceptions, by means of the senses.

The consciousness of sensory experience postulates a science of the "I" (or a Philosophy of Freedom). Solar spiritual practice leads us to experience the content of perception's extraneousness to the activity of the sensory organ by means of which it manifests. When it takes place in the sensory organ, during perception, it is only explained by the presence of the "I." The perceptive process, as a process of the physical organ, is extraneous to the real content, just as the telephonic apparatus has nothing to do with the content of a conversion, nor with the corresponding voices.

The sensory organ does not serve to transmit sensory contents to the human body endowed with a sentient soul.

Rather, it serves to give the "I" a way to gather such contents, as relations that already exist between sentient corporeality and the world (relations that subsist even without the presence of the "I") as is the case with animals.

The "I" gathers, in perception, its own presence in the world. The lack of a more radical, or a more individual activity of consciousness, which enables it to notice this gathering of its own presence—or its own power—in the world, by means of perception, renders the life of the senses overwhelming as the domain of an immediate multiplicity, which cannot be overcome by the weak contraposition that is unifying, numerical and logical.

The sensory image of the world rises by way of the suprasensory power of perceiving—not to the extent that the world's content is illusory, or subjectively existent, but to the extent that, through perceiving, it assumes the form that appears as reality. Pure perceiving leads the spiritual practitioner to the thresholds of the "I" that perceives, namely, to the "I" always presupposed, but never seen—the force that we presuppose and never are. With pure perceiving, the spiritual practitioner becomes part of the process of profound concentration, wherein flows the force of the Higher "I." We normally flee from this force by passing from one perception to another, always evading its penetration, continually attracted by the longing of sensations. The spiritual practitioner separates perceiving from sensation. But we must have already sufficiently trained conscious attention by means of the concentration exercise.

Pure Perceiving

Visual impressions typically lend themselves to the practice of pure perceiving, whose process, once possessed, can later be extended to all sensations, with a gradualness that goes from the most conscious sensations to those that are less conscious, such as smell, taste, touch, etc.

As a preparation, it is helpful to turn to objects whose nature allows one to easily separate the inner content from sensation—for example, crystals, metals, plants, flowers, water, sky, the relation of light between a plant and the background of the sky. The operation consists in contemplating the object, with utmost attention and, at the same time, with total silence of thought, until becoming absolutely immobile before it. Sensation and mental pictures must become silent. In the presence of nature's creation, immobility spontaneously passes over into profound quiet. This quiet is that of the power of universal thinking, which manifests in etheric-physical forms.

The object becomes the imaginative symbol of a specific creative current of nature. In contemplative continuity, we encounter the suprasensory structures of whose formative power the object is a sign. Such structures rise up in our soul as a force of images ("images-force"). The operation gradually becomes clear and intense, going on to coincide with the dynamics of the relationship of the "I" to the sensory realm from which springs the physical "appearing" of the world.

As we have seen, the relation of the "I" is direct. Therefore, in pure perceiving we learn the art of gathering the movements of the soul's life, before they acquire form, or become sensation. In essence, we overcome cerebral mediation with respect to the contents of thinking, feeling, and willing. We can begin the act of controlling and integrating such contents, by grasping them in their pure state, unaltered by the subjective element.

To actualize the pure relation of the "I" independent of the astral body, teaches us many things—the detachment from our own karma as well as that of others, by ascending to the sphere of freedom from which it is possible to contemplate the current of karma and to cooperate in its positive fulfillment. This is true ethics—the spirit's autonomy in human action, for a profound action within the human being; the possibility of grasping the original element of thinking, feeling, and willing, in movement, before it extinguishes itself in dialectical consciousness; the possibility of operating in them before they become destructive within the psyche and within human relations.

The inner process of perceiving, as we have mentioned, can be gradually extended to all perceptions—all the way to those that are inner, subjective, or psychic, that is to say, all the way to instinctive impulses, and ultimately to sex. However, it is wise to gradually penetrate the types of perception, from those that are more independent to those tied to physical corporeality.

We will understand that the art of experiencing, in sex, the highest soul forces, and thus, real purification, is the separating of perception from sensation. True spagyria consists of such a separation—an art more subtle than that required by the simple perception of forms, colors, sounds, etc., because its inner content reveals itself to be immediately identical to that of an erotic sensation. The path indicated in this manual provides a way of realizing pure perceiving in that sense, so that the will's pure warmth can be grasped (see "The Power of Eros").

THE POWER OF IMAGINATION

As pupils, we create an objective force out of imagination by utilizing the power of spontaneity proper to its immediate form—a power that is normally subjective, because it does not move according to its own inner principle but, rather, by deviating from this, in accordance with the sentient soul's demand, or that of our psycho-physiological nature.

Imagination is a force that tends toward its own realization, in accordance with the impulse that truly moves it from the depths. Such an impulse can be creative; it can be destructive. Ordinarily, it is destructive, because it ascends from the sentient soul, namely, from the soul instinctively opposed to its own suprasensory source. There is no imagining that is not the germ of a reality on the way to realizing itself. The germ is almost always moved by an impulse that is directly opposite to the original nature of thinking. Ordinary imagining is such an impulse expressing itself as immediate thinking, namely, mental picturing. This mental picturing, however, can be directed by the will and empowered by means of non-subjective contents. The spiritual practitioner will learn that no creation lacks, as its initial germ, the imaginative power of thinking—insofar as it frees itself from subjectivity.

Usually, imagining is dynamic, thanks to the willful spontaneous (or instinctive) element, which is congenial to it, insofar as it is bound to our psycho-physiological nature and is, therefore, subjective. The pupil, tending to free the volitive element of imaging from nature, so as to make an objective force of it, encounters this very difficulty. The imagining's flow loses the power of spontaneity when its form is determined by consciousness. Determinately willed, it loses the force that it naturally bears within itself. The art of the spiritual practitioner consists in reviving the imaginative impulse by means of the will, namely, in reconnecting its flow to the original force by making a current of will out of spontaneity, as it effectively is in the beginning.

The discipline of imagination is cultivated by devoting attention to given mental pictures, until such pictures arouse a specific feeling. Mental picturing is an initial imagining, normally used by the sentient soul, or the emotional rational-soul. Nonetheless, mental picturing is the initial movement of imaginative thinking. It must, by way of discipline, free itself of the feeling that subtly conditions it, in order to give rise to that feeling which corresponds to the imagining aroused.

The imaginative faculty is trained: *a)* by allowing the images of the human being's cosmic history, described by the Spiritual Science, to act upon it, based on a state of contemplative immobility; *b)* by contemplating mineral or vegetative nature (see "Pure Perceiving"); *c)* by fashioning an image according to a given spiritual content and contemplating it—thereby nourishing its movement; d) when imagining a color, by abstracting from the sensory structure through which it normally manifests, so as to contemplate its non-sensory content. We can later imagine the combination of two colors—e.g. red and blue—and perceive their subtle relationship, which must rise up alive. We must ensure that each image achieves its fulfillment within the soul, by resounding with a given feeling. This feeling opens the passage to the spiritual, which reaches right down to the physical.

The imaginative discipline involves the most ample power of choice and independent use of images, turned toward the rigorous control of a force to which it must, nevertheless, simultaneously allow the greatest freedom of manifestation. It is appropriate to speak of conscious will. The expression of the imaginative *dynamis* is essentially a mediation offered to the flowing of the highest inner life, to whose impersonality an adequate opening in the soul is assured, by the limitless mobility.

With the flowing of such a force, we make life's inner element our own, which is identical to that of creative nature. We have at our disposal the initial form of inner Magic. One can say that it is the Magic of the new times, because it is founded on the soul's internal logic—the germ of the human being's conscious redemption and of a real evolution of ethic-social processes, insofar as it corresponds in our consciousness to the archetypal power of the concept, namely, to the principal of the original synthesis of normal thought. It is the imagining that ancient spiritual practitioners did not need to liberate, since it was not bound to the nervous system, but flowed to them gratuitously from the same psychosomatic condition. Their art was to donate themselves to it, or to sink into it, or to escape by means of it.

For modern pupils the opposite task arises, namely, to free the imagination from the psychosomatic condition. With this, we experience within ourselves a cosmic process. We can say that what exists, worldwide and humanly, is the condensation—to the point of minerality—of powerful superhuman imaginations, according to cosmic archetypes. Such imaginations, naturally, have behind them creative powers even more profound, namely, those of the cosmic Entities' Inspiration and Intuition. We just barely begin to comprehend a plant, if we recognize within it the realized imagination of a superhuman thought. In fact, we can, at the very most, translate our own objective power of image into a machine, which is a lifeless object, just as our ordinary imaginative thought is lifeless—insofar as it is not experienced beyond cerebralism.

Thus, sickness is an extra-conscious imagination, incarnated. It has, at its root, an intense imagination that is correlated to the corporeal state, by means of which the spirit tends toward a given attainment. Such imagination, possessed, is the principle of healing. Those of us capable of imagining the realization of our own healing, already set the healing force into motion. Naturally, we must be guided by self-knowledge and, therefore, knowledge of the karmic reasons for our illness. If we manage to recognize the metaphysical causes of illness, we can work on ourselves. It has to do, however, with a recognition that differs greatly from that of psychic analysis. Also along lines of such an investigation, the technique consists in enlivening given key-images by way of repetition and rhythm.

Those who intend to give autonomy to creative imagination, must, above all, know the art of concentration and of meditation. We free imagination from the astral body (*kama rupa*) so as to direct it with the maximum power of control. Such control, however, as we have mentioned, is what normally extinguishes its power of spontaneity. But it is precisely this spontaneity that we tend to assume as the astral body's vehicle of revivification, so that this astral body, in turn, expresses the highest imaginative power.

In willed imagining, something intimate is at work, something more powerful than the imagining itself. Free imagining is activated by means of the will, rather than by a willful exertion, which paralyzes its force. An image becomes dynamic when it can be contemplated disinterestedly, like a painting already completed. We must will with maximum force, but with an absolute absence of determination, with a non-willing of the Taoist kind. Naturally, this does not mean according to the Taoist discipline but, rather, by virtue of an incorporeal movement of thinking that is as intense as if it were corporeal—namely, according to the Rosicrucian discipline of thinking.

Imagination is trained by means of concentration and meditation. If we observe, concentration is essentially an exercise of imagination. Likewise, meditation is the "imagining" that connects thinking with the subtle forces of feeling and willing, according to their original harmony.

Those of us who, as spiritual practitioners, possess this "imagining" have the principal of Divine Magic. All self-realization becomes possible to us by means of the rhythmic and repeated imaginative exercise. Whoever feels lacking in forces of devotion, can imagine devotion, its power, its content, and the transformation of one's own inner life, thanks to its emergence. The consecration of oneself to the spiritual world always begins as an intense imagination. In effect, there is no inner realization, which is not, above all, an imaginative *opus*.

For decisive inner operations, "imagining" must draw from its cosmic origin. Only in this way does it become pure; it frees itself of the subtle egoic impulses that, of necessity, it hides within itself. If these were not eliminated, they would give rise to demonic imaginative magic. As spiritual practitioners, we must possess pure thinking and be familiar with the path of knowledge in order not to come up against the mediumistic paths of egoic imagining.

Above all, we each realize what we truly imagine. We find outside ourselves what we imaginatively nourish within ourselves. Impure human beings cannot but encounter impurity, outside their very selves. The pure person always encounters what is pure.

The thinking that we truly think is not rational. Rather, it is the thinking that bears a charge of life; it is the "imagining." Normally, however, it is the "imagining" of the sentient soul or of the astral body, that is to say, of the soul obligated to resound according to corporeality. Rational thought is always the codifier of what we really think according to the instinctive charge of life. Usually this charge of life comes from subjective feeling, from the psyche, from corporeal nature. Our task is to make it spring forth from the source of life itself. We must restore the objective power of life to the "imagining."

It is not an outer situation that arouses the psychic state, but the psychic state that projects itself into an outer situation. In that sense, imagination is the creative force. It can create illness, error, worry and longing by giving power to what destroys the soul and the body. Physical illness, as previously mentioned, is an unconscious imagination, realized. But whereas destructive "imagining" has an immediate force that comes from nature, namely, from the *ego* that is one with nature, imagination that is creative, or elevating, or curative demands the conscious determination of willing. This determination initially involves effort, as in freeing mental picturing from the psychophysical limit. But the effort is gradually eliminated so that pure imaging—with its limitless power of spontaneity—can free itself of subjective nature.

One can say that the spiritual world nourishes the living by means of powerful imaginations. Human imagining is nothing but the lower projection of such imagining. As modern human beings, we render imagination egoic and subjective. We can build castles in the air. But, in practical terms, we only create machines. Even on an aesthetic level, we now produce nothing but a cerebral art, devoid of the living element, that is to say, devoid of real imagining.

As has been mentioned, concentration or meditation exercises work toward liberating the "imagining." If such liberation is achieved, our responsibility toward ourselves and toward others becomes serious, for the fact that imagination, as an initial magical force, can destroy if it is wrongly used, or if it escapes the control of the operator, to the extent that it is grasped again by our egoic nature. We can gravely damage ourselves, as well as others, if, during moments of low self-awareness, we lose control of the imaginative force that is awakened.

The reason that the spiritual world does not grant us specific powers is because of the danger that we, not having attained real independence from our egoic nature, can make of their use. When imaginative power is awakened, our life must be a continuous control of its very spontaneity—even in the minutest details— so that this power does not become a force adverse to human evolution.

The Exercise of the Rose Cross

The exercise of the Rose Cross communicated for the first time by Rudolf Steiner (see *Esoteric Science*, ch. 4), briefly consists in imagining the birth and formation of a plant, and in comparing this to the image of the human being. As human beings, we lack the purity and the impersonality of the plant. The fact that we are endowed with consciousness and the autonomy of action implies, as a counterpart, our subjection to instincts and to passions. However, by means of spiritual practice, we can attain in the soul—and, therefore, in the body—the same purity that characterizes the plant. We can realize in the blood, whose warmth is the vehicle of instincts and passions, the same purity that circulates in the green juice of the plant. At this point in the exercise, the red rose is assumed as the symbol of the spiritual practitioner's metaphysical transformation. In such a flower, the green juice turns red in the petals. This image is to be intensely felt (see "Meditation"). Then, suddenly, we imagine a black cross, as the symbol of purified passions and instincts, with seven bright red roses at its center, in a circle. Such a definitive image must be contemplated, so that it can offer the feeling that belongs to it.

If we observe, the exercise involves thinking, feeling and willing. It reassumes the operations of concentration, of meditation and of imagination. Through the metaphysical contents to which it imaginatively appeals, the exercise can lead us very far, regardless of the level at which we find ourselves, if we accompany it during the day with the exercise typical of concentration and eventually with secondary disciplines necessary to our personal development. At a particular stage, the exercise—elevated to the calm intensity capable of penetrating the lower astral and of orienting the life of the soul—can lead us to a connection with the invisible Order that guides humanity, known as the Brotherhood of the Rose Cross.

The Power of Distraction

It is the power of removing the mental sphere from a thought or from an invading mood. Such a power is cultivated by the practice of suddenly passing from one course of thought—in which we are particularly engrossed—to another for which we have no interest and in which we willingly immerse ourselves to the point of allowing ourselves to be taken by it: then repeating an analogous distraction with a further course of thoughts—just as with a feeling, or with a mood. The exercise practically consists of devoting ourselves to a thought or to an alluring feeling, until reaching a verifiable phase of subjection to it. We then immediately leave it, in order to dedicate ourselves to another non-alluring thought or feeling—in which we become engrossed with the same self-devotion.

All of that by which we are taken without being able to do without, is evil, even if it has to do with impulses that are seemingly spiritual. When authentic, an impulse of goodness or of morality does not govern the "I," for it is an expression of the "I." Even a spiritual impulse must pass through the sieve of conscious determination.

The impulses of goodness and generosity can be recognized as authentic, when they are the transformation of the astral body's lower impulses. They constitute a meaningful soul life, in which the real "I" is essentially expressed. The presence of this real "I" in the world is already a transformative action. Any form of this action is a relation of the "I," which must not run away with the "I." The virtue of the relation comes from the spirit. It cannot come from moralistic exaltation, which is almost always a pretense, or recitation of the spirit.

The exercise of willful distraction has the task of freeing the soul not only from the forces adverse to the spiritual (Ahriman), but also from those of spiritual recitation (Lucifer).

Even the use of a moral impulse can become illicit, if it is not the decision of the "I" but, rather, of the astral body's longing. The science of morality is, above all, a science of freedom, namely, a science of the "I." The world's true ills are the product of a morality used not by the "I," but by its opposite—a morality to which there is nothing to object, dialectically. Rather, it is essentially the deceiver of human beings, and the organizer of their systematic alienation, insofar as it is merely formal; its systematic content does not come from the spirit of fraternity but, rather, from the spirit of aversion.

The exercise of distraction is the catharsis of the forces that appear by means of concentration. The power that results from concentration must be connected with the impersonal direction of the "I." By such a path, we learn the change of polarity necessary for passing from subjective (or mental) concentration, to the profound concentration that bears the impersonality of the Higher "I."

When we are strong enough, we can attempt a more demanding form of the exercise, by willfully becoming engrossed in a tormenting thought, until we manage to perceive its illusory and tormenting content. Having thus reached saturation, we suddenly detach from this in order to immerse ourselves in a thought with an opposing content. With this content, we accomplish the same operation, which is to strengthen the formal structure until penetrating its content. The exercise is to be concluded by inwardly comparing the two contents, for whose evocation an identical force is put in motion.

Along the same lines, a further exercise can be the following. We imagine a situation that normally brings about a given sentiment, as its irresistible correlation, and we train ourselves to avoid such a sentiment, by imaginatively countering the situation with a state of absolute imperturbability.

This exercise, which would seem to cultivate a kind of egoistic insensibility, serves, instead, to awaken the sensibility toward situations that normally leave us indifferent, insofar as they do not contradict the *ego*. There are neutral or obtuse zones of the soul in which the most profound opposition to the spirit is rooted. We arrive at them by controlling the sensitivity by means of which they normally influence the *ego*.

The part of the soul that remains imperturbable because of its obtuseness, normally maintains its power by means of the part that reacts in the form of emotions and passions. In relation to this, we can understand the importance of training ourselves to consider the situations of others as if they were our own, and our own as if they concerned others. The value of such an exercise is not so much the moral content, as it is the technique of its *dynamis*.

The light of the force requires a logic regarding the soul's movements, which is as rigorous as that of a mathematical theorem. Spontaneity is the creative power, endowed with infinity, which involves overcoming the given, but, therefore, first of all, the possession of rigorous determinateness.

INSTINCTS

Instinct is an impulse within the depths of the psyche that appears authoritative, despite the "I." Actually, it manages to use the "I." The group of instincts that governs from the will sphere or from the profound astral is what truly arises as a human force—the greatest force at our disposal. Thought bears within itself the light of reason, instinct's transformative idea, but it lacks the force of instinct. The art of concentration and of meditation consists in fortifying thought, so that it can come to have the power of an instinct. This thinking becomes a dynamic synthesis of feeling and willing, which, thanks to the discipline, are essentially withdrawn from the dynamics of the instincts.

The problem of the "I"-being's autonomy with respect to instincts, is a problem of the "I"-being's relationship with the potential forces of the real human state—an overwhelming instinct is a destructive force of such a state. A dominated instinct becomes an edifying force, or better yet, a decisive force. It is easy to realize that the autonomy with respect to instincts is not extemporized. It can begin take shape on secure foundations, thanks to concentration and to meditation.

When a minimum of inner independence is attained, we can train ourselves to operate through instincts by using their power. It is a matter of integrating ourselves into this power, as if into something willed. By means of the "imaginative" technique, we prepare for it, by evoking a given instinct. Intuitive speed and imaginative power are needed, in order to catch sight of the instinctive current that is evoked and to plunge into it—not being dragged by it but, rather, overcoming it, by going beyond, by adding an element of guiding will to the current that already exists. It is a matter of training the dynamic imagination and the subtle perception, in order to grasp the instinctive current and lead it beyond itself. Instinct is damaging because it pursues the "I" and submerges it. The art is to introduce a more powerful "I" into the instinctive current, namely, to insert a "furthermore" of the "I" into the lower impulse, so as to overturn its direction. It has to do with a sort of inner *judo*, that not only readies the control over instincts on behalf of the "I," but their rebirth as direct powers of the spirit. The power of instincts can again become the instrument of the "I."

This possibility is also prepared by means of will exercises. The will is strengthened through the discipline of concentration and of meditation, but it can be brought to a tenor of strength through the exercise of pure action, which consists of imposing duties not called for by our everyday *routine*. Such actions, entirely simple and of little importance, are to be realized through careful compliance between prearrangement and execution: all the more effective if between prearrangement and execution a certain stretch of time—let us say, twenty-four hours—elapses. A weak-willed personality is decisively strengthened by the self-imposition of a series of commands for actions to be carried out for their own sake, even from one hour of the day to another—in order to avoid intervals of inertia or of the lethargic dispersion of forces.

The Master of the new times gives specific preparatory exercises of the power capable of working upon instincts in a transformative way. One, for example, is to re-evoke the impressions received from an individual taken by desire, and to depict it to oneself so as to be able to perceive something more of what was experienced on that occasion. By doing so, we can observe how longing works upon our behavior and upon our physiognomy; we can feel longing, but within that person. In this way, we evoke that longing within us and at the same time control it, for we depersonalize it and feel it to be objective. The completion of such an exercise consists in re-evoking the individual that was satisfied by the longing and is, thus, inwardly happy and relaxed. To feel this satisfaction, by remaining independent of its harmful aspect, is a further active penetration into the sphere of instincts.

The Exercise of Memory

The conscious re-evocation of given impressions and inner situations of the past can become the contemplation of a process of forces which had then involved the soul and which can now instead rise up to reveal their objective content. The mnemonic contemplation also becomes a connection with the "supra-feel-able" forces of the rhythmic center (thorax), as well as the possibility of the breath's initial autonomy from the nervous system. The exercise essentially gives rise to the presence of the higher "I" within the rhythm of the etheric body. It corresponds, therefore, to a subtle experience of time, insofar as it is an etheric current independent of the spatial-sensory form in which it manifests.

The exercise consists in re-evoking an event, or a past situation, in order to extract from it the mood that was connected with it. Then, one isolates the mood from the corresponding sensory phenomenology and contemplates it objectively, just as one contemplates the final content of concentration at the completion of the exercise. The deliberate reproduction of an inner content tends to reenliven a profound element of will, which in the past experience was indeed present, but subconscious and, therefore, unable to be assimilated. In the conscious re-evocation, the profound volitive element is perceived. It becomes reintegrated, as an instinctive power, by the higher forces of consciousness.

The exercise of remembering past experiences gives us a way to perceive the weaving of time as a rhythm of the etheric body, until it springs from the higher astral body's sphere of "musicality." This musicality enchants the instincts' serpentine element. In reality, we intervene in the pure inner content of the remembered event, now subconsciously present, and transform it into a content of consciousness, by realizing a profound redeeming action of the instinctive sphere. Moreover, we strengthen ordinary memory by way of such a path.

Calm

Calm is a state of peace with beings and with events—regardless of what they are—that realizes the true nature of the soul. It is a legitimate state of peace if, above all, it is actualized when motives of contrast, or reasons of disapproval, are ethically justified. Essentially, it is the possibility of eliminating the spirit of aversion, which is inseparable even from the ethical expression of the *ego*. Without overcoming the spirit of aversion, real calm is not possible, nor, therefore, is the spiritual path. We must emphasize that precisely such a state of peace with beings—despite conflicts—enables situations to evolve and transforms human attitudes.

Calm is easy for those of us who do not react to the evil and error of the world, having at our disposal a capacity for agreement and for positive co-existence with it. This calm, however, is not a force of the soul but, rather, of the soul governed by nature—a state of obtuseness, which feigns the force of the soul.

Even the most careful disciples can be torn asunder by indignation, and momentarily lose calm, when they chance upon displays of dishonesty, or of wickedness, or of immorality. The correction of these (displays) and the corresponding severity are just, but always ruined by the spirit of aversion that accompanies them. We must separate the spirit of aversion from them, by transforming it into a force that cognitively penetrates the phenomenon. The separation is a form of spagyria that is fundamental to viewing the backdrop of human struggles, and fundamental to a healthy inner development. Without calm amidst the tumult, no suprasensory experience can occur, nor can there exist the possibility of being just, as well as helpful, toward our neighbors.

The spirit of aversion can be truly confronted when it legitimately manifests together with justified sentiments of disapproval of what is unjust and contemptible. To observe oneself and to remove the impulse of hatred from these sentiments bestows the correct development upon them. It makes them vehicles of a curative rectification. A technique of Spiritual Science consists in training oneself to direct the impulse of hatred toward the spirit of error and of lies, by diverting it from the person who is its vehicle. It is methodologically important to train oneself to become aware of another's point of view, and in that sense, to justify it.

When the impulse of hatred, which attempts to surface in legitimate indignation, is controlled, we can behold with understanding the event or the people who arouse disapproval. This understanding calms the soul. Such calm is the correlation, which, as we have mentioned, occultly allows the event, or another person's attitude, to evolve.

Calm realizes the soul's true nature. No movement of the soul is authentic, if it lacks its essential quality—calm. Calm arises, if we manage to see in those who execute shameful actions, individuals possessed by Entities of which the meditative discipline provides a way of becoming free. As experimenters, we discover that we can free ourselves of them, because others undergo their subjection. The ultimate sense of this is that we feel the responsibility to understand and help those who endure the sacrifice of subjection—of whose overcoming we are privileged to possess the inner technique.

Understanding and forgiving everyone—no one excluded—as well as accepting and tolerating unjust situations, must arise from knowledge. As attitudes and sentimental positions, they hold up little, even when they are not pretenses. As attainments of penetrating thought, they are the vehicles of true calm, namely, of the inner state from which, alone, there can arise the energies of an action that repairs and eliminates error.

Conscious peace is attained, above all, thanks to the cognitive penetration of events and of beings that cause our condemnation and, consequently, our aversion to be more severe. Just as we cannot feel aversion toward a phenomenon of nature, so too, can we not feel aversion toward an event of karma. What, originating from others, can arouse disapproval or disdain is always a product of karma—that is, of instinctive impulses and of temperament, for which beings are led to given actions or to a given behavior. It does not come from their free spirit. To justify everyone according to *dharma*—the law that governs them by means of karma and the corresponding persuasion of being within truth—creates a sense of relaxation and peace with beings, which is the principle of the soul's autonomy. Only the soul has the power to heal human injustice and error without partiality or factitiousness. A just severity cannot help but do without the perception of the inner behind-the-scenes-activity. It can only come from the calm of knowing, and from understanding the true motives of human subjects.

Calm, united with the comprehensive contemplation of an unpleasant event, secretly corrects the error. It develops the forces of fraternity beyond displays of dissent and struggle. We must be at peace with everyone, so that we can know the Threshold of the soul's life. "Everything goes as it should go" is the wisdom from which the pupil draws the underlying calm. The art is not to oppose, in an unseemly manner, what happens, or propose to impede what happens, but to work at removing the causes for which unpleasant things occur. These causes are, however, always spiritual and they are to be removed through spiritual action at their point of origin. The real harm of the present day lies in the lack of original operators, namely, the lack of action that moves on the plane of causes. It is truly the most arduous task. Those who really dedicate themselves to this action achieve a higher state of calm, necessary as inspiration to the tasks of the usual operators.

Technically, calm is the spontaneous state of the soul, when the soul actualizes its real nature—independent of corporeality. If it can in such a way be perceived as an objective entity, calm must be left to act as a natural state to which we previously were unconsciously opposed. It can be intensified to the point where nothing in the world can remove it. This unalterable calm must be known as a prerequisite to real suprasensory experience.

In certain moments, we must pick ourselves up in inner silence and let the calm of what we originally are, descend—free of human attitudes. We must be as we are, until tensions are exhausted—tensions that truly do not exist for the "I," but only for what the "I" is not. Calm is the foundation from which we continually move without knowing it. To be is already to be calm. It is a matter of knowing it. It is a matter of being what we are at the foundation.

Rosicrucian Method

Calm must be possible at any moment, in all circumstances. We must be able to evoke it on command. For this, we must meticulously be prepared. We must possess the state of autonomy and detachment that results from intense concentration. This state of autonomy and detachment, evoked, should be continually sufficient to restore calm.

If the situation is so overwhelming that such self-command is only partially or superficially possible, then the Rosicrucian method of retreating into the essence of the astral body is advisable. In simplified terms, the art is to "receive," to yield, to abandon oneself totally—to not resist. Resisting is a mistake.

Let us again recall the concept of inner *judo*. It has nothing to do with an instrumental image but, rather, with a precise technique, which appeals to forces that are present today in the astral body's relation to the "I," and which, therefore, has nothing in common with *judo* in the strict sense of the word. Any form of agitation, in essence, is but the illegitimate prevailing of astral impulses over the "I." If they did not control the "I," these impulses would manifest as its forces.

What we conveniently call inner *judo* is a technique foreseen by the ancient solar spiritual practice, in that it is a discipline that restores the original movement of the astral, which utilizes the forces of alteration within the alteration itself. This technique consists in abandoning oneself even more profoundly to agitation, beyond what is its hold upon the soul, until being able to add a volitive force to the impulsive current.

We must not forget that, within the soul, will and impulsivity are the same force under a different rule. The initial movement is to escape capture, namely, to surrender beyond the very limit of alienated calm; it is to insert ourselves here, or to insert the imaginative-volitive current already trained by means of exercises, so as to descend into the profound zone within us, where the original forge of forces exists.

To abandon ourselves, to yield subtly, to free ourselves and simultaneously operate as we would in *judo*, is, from an occult point of view, to operate with the permanent forces of the Buddha, which today cosmically enliven, within human depths, the capacity of freedom from the sensory realm within sensory experience. The Buddha's original contribution, directed in antiquity toward sparing the spiritual practitioner the conditions of sensory experience, today becomes the soul's positive impulse grasped by the sensory realm. In that sense, the Buddhistic processes within the soul today express their true function. They collaborate in the action of the essence-Logos within the "I." They open the path to the Christ.

The limit of alienated calm can be reached by means of the most profound forces of the "I," evoked by the state of necessity, that is, by agitation. Usually, they work toward the unconscious restabilization of calm at the expense of the etheric-physical organism. Such calm is fictitious, because it does not spring from the "I"-being's willful action within the astral, but from an insufficiency of the "I" with respect to such action. Therefore, it confirms that dependence of the astral on the lower nature, which will reproduce the agitation.

The inner *judo* manages to free the "I"-being's most radical forces by means of a sinking that is willed in the alienated calm, which is to say, by means of the very forces of agitation that automatically involve the "I." We must possess this automatism. It is the transference of function from instinctiveness to imaginative will, possible as a *judo*-like yielding. It corresponds to the attitude, "God's Will be done," technically brought to its last resort.

Usually, this attitude is a passivity of inertia. We must take it further, from the essence, all the way to the power of inert passivity. To lead this passivity beyond itself is to descend into the depths, until reaching the entire root of the being that organically rules physical corporeality. It is a fundamental presence of the "I," from one of its more elevated attained heights.

True calm is reached, when it becomes the soul's golden zone. There, we can retreat, as if it were a magical landscape, in order to become independent of conditions when these become overwhelming—like actors that leave the scene where they are reciting a difficult role with which they identify and discover themselves, realizing the functional unreality of the world that they have just left, that is, an unreality whose human measure consists of pain and death. Of these, living calm truly realizes the metaphysical content—profound peace.

Outside such a possibility, the issue of calm nevertheless remains when the cause of that for which calm is lost persists, when agitation is due to a situation of fact that does not change, or is aggravated, or is waiting for us at a given time. For this situation, one can refer to what is said in the paragraphs that regard "Karma," "The Power of Distraction," and the redemption of "Instincts," respectively.

Soul Ataraxia

Soul ataraxia is the experience that results from that of absolute calm. It is the possibility of contemplating the world's evil without residual sentiments of condemnation or aversion, and of responding with the pure relation of the knowledge and donation of oneself—the precondition of Initiation. It is the metaphysical immobility from which springs the astral body's maximum force.

Essentially, it is the radical presence of the higher "I," which is realized in the bodily sphere as the immobility of the nervous system with respect to the astral that moves by means of it, because of its relation with consciousness (see "The Spiritual Practice of Feeling"). The more the nervous system alienates itself from the astral world, the more its original force springs from this astral world.

Metaphysical immobility is the work of the "I." However, as the immobility of the nervous system, it is mediated by the same astral body, there, where in the cerebral mental sphere it has a direct hold on the nervous system by way of thought. Arresting the flow of thoughts as well as mental silence are therefore the beginning. It is helpful to remember that there does not exist a higher astral body experience that is not an experience of the "I."

An authentic experience of the astral is always an experience of the "I." The "I," however, is the Subject—the unseen experimenter of the astral. In the same way that a big carp does not lose itself in limpid or murky water but rather finds itself to be the ruler of its own element, so, too, does the "I" not lose itself in the astral world—neither higher nor lower. Rather, the "I" moves securely within it. The more it is immersed in it, the more it governs it.

The ataraxia of the astral is that experience of the "I" at the heart of the soul's life, which in another paragraph we call the vortex of immobile power, or the whirling immobility. It realizes the zero of the astral body's bond with the sensory. In effect, it reawakens its original nature in the astral body. If we bear in mind that this bond is what renders it destructive with regards to the physical and etheric bodies and the higher currents of the "I," we can understand how the annihilation of the bond that is mediated by the silent mental sphere, is the principle of Solar Magic. One can understand the sense of Rosicrucian meditation, as the contemplation of the plant's pure astral—pure and primordial, since it is not incarnated in the plant. It is how the astral of the spiritual practitioner should be, despite being incarnated.

What we truly lack is not the force of the "I," which is overabundant in forms of the *ego*. What we are truly missing is the relationship of the "I" with the astral body—or (the relationship) of the original soul—in which we are blindly immersed, so as to use it as a body of desire, nevertheless being always overwhelmed by it. In reality, it is always—like the "I"—used by the astral body, whose real nature is divine.

Creative abnegation is the ataraxia of the astral, willfully realized. It is a detachment from the value of appearances, which has nothing to do with quietism or tamasic inertia, to the extent that it is the force of pacification in the depths—an overwhelming whirlwind for all that is sensual and inert, namely, rajasic or tamasic.

Radical appeasement is the absolute independence from the "appearing"—namely, the limitless immersing into oneself. It is like letting oneself sink into an abyss, to which no connection with the body or the psyche can be opposed. It is an absolute "descending" that ignores all impediments. One frees oneself of all impurities. One frees oneself of all suffering, according to the power of an original non-being, which is the true being. In reality, one operates within the physical body by exhausting the need of the physical support, all the way to a radical extraneousness from what we are, constitutionally. In this extraneousness, we receive the force that governs the psyche and the body.

The operation is a disarticulating of the soul's constitutional ill, which is essentially desire. The descent into the depths is the gradually more subtle liberation of the astral body's lower vehicles. Such vehicles continually reproduce the inversion of its original forces, for which the force of love becomes hatred, and the capacity of donation becomes desire. A psychophysical regeneration is possible, but on condition that one has the courage to restore the astral to its original purity, which is precisely a descent into the empty depths, devoid of support that is not the pure force of the "I."

It is the courage to descend into the abyss, within whose depths one finds absolute stability without support. It has nevertheless to do with courage that can spring from a preparation of the qualitative element of the spiritual practice—the consecration of the Work, which involves morality, fidelity, and continuity.

The Rosicrucian path is characterized by a profound experience of the soul, or of the true astral body, by means of the axial power of the "I" (see "The Power of the Cross"). In particular, the Rosicrucian exercise opens the threshold to the experience of the divine astral, or of the soul's innermost weaving, unknown to normal consciousness. In reality, we bear within us the Kingdom of Heaven, but we ignore it. We do not lack the central impulse of the "I" but, rather, the crucial experience of the "I" within the soul. We lack the experience of the "Virgin," or of Isis Sophia and, consequently, of the soul's real androgynous nature. The pure vehicular force of the "I" is normally corrupted as dialectical consciousness.

Prayer

Just as meditation is the process that elevates the soul to the Divine, to the ends of the Divine itself, prayer is this elevation according to human request. This request, however, is a pure ideal determination. If it is a request of the psyche or of the egoic mental sphere, it makes no sense.

The ideal determination is turned toward the Divine, equally as a proposal and support to its action. The determination's ideal force is the level of overcoming the subjective (or egoic) limit, so that prayer can acquire the power of objectification. Prayer, bound to the *ego*, has no power. If it achieves its objective, despite its egoic bond, this is the concession of powers belonging to a subsensory order, which help, provided that they govern the petitioner's soul according to lower magic that is diametrically opposite to Solar Magic. In that way, a "pact" is established from whose consequences the human "contractor" has difficulty removing him or herself.

We can pray with traditional prayers, or, even more effectively, with simple profound intent. This profound intent, which is a "praying" without words, is more difficult to realize, because, lacking dialectical support, it can easily become a confused jumble of thoughts and sentiments, incapable of overcoming the subjective limit. True intent demands being brought to the purity of impetus, of lucidity, and of continuity, so as to actualize the communion to which the certainty of the Divine's response is inseparable.

When we pray without words—according to a profound intent—thinking, feeling and willing are elevated according to a single idea, which must attain the intensity of the concentration, in order to maintain the purity and continuity necessary to the force's objectification. At a given moment, within the spiritual practitioner's force of elevation, moves the force of the Divine, which is evoked.

We must leave the use of prayer's mediation to the Divine, so that it can decide its form. The form of what is demanded in prayer must be determined not by the speaking spiritual practitioner, but by the forces to which we turn. It is important that we do not ask anything for ourselves that has not been suggested to us by these same forces. We can begin with prayer, so that what we must ask can be suggested to us, if we don't intuit it directly. But the most effective prayer is that without an object, which really operates by way of the Divine and, consequently, by way of the human community.

Prayer is the human mediation for the variations of collective karma. Therefore, its ultimate content has to do with the radical forces of the will, by means of which individual karma expresses itself. The mystical power of prayer is, in fact, the power of depersonalized will. As a higher form of Solar Magic, capable of soliciting the developed variations of karma, prayer involves the connection with the Solar principle, or with the Christ, known in Rosicrucian terms as the "Lord of Karma." Therefore, intense prayer, without an object, is the most powerful type of prayer.

The connection between prayer and the spiritual practitioner's *opus* is attainable, if we understand that meditating is the highest form of prayer and that whatever lights up as the light of life in meditation is indeed aroused through the initiative of the "I." This, however, is possible only to the extent that the decision of the spiritual world responds to such an initiative.

We can connect to the ascetic-magical *opus*, if we notice that the forces of prayer pass through the arms and hands, and that hands joined in prayer are the conductors of the powers of prayer. The hands think and feel more devoutly than individual thinking and feeling, because the Supra-individual in them expresses itself directly, without depending on cerebral mediation. Through them, an evocative wisdom passes that ordinary thought has yet to possess. The hands open and close a circuit of force, in which the infinite power of the Cosmos is present. They can bless and heal, because the soul, better than the so-called magnetic force—the inferior dynamism of nature still (save rare exceptions) opposed to the spirit—bears the cosmic soul through them.

As spiritual practitioners, we have already found the path of reintegration when our whole life is a continuous profound prayer, and when we feel the force that works toward healing the ills of the world flow in joined hands. The task of prayer is to lift humanity from the state of sordidness, prosaicness, and animality, so that the soul can cognize the part of itself that is immersed in physical corporeality and is, therefore, unknown, namely, the divine soul, the wisdom of love, or the Virgin Sophia, which is continually removed from it through its identification with corporeality.

The image of the Virgin is the symbol of prayer's profound intent, namely, the donation of all of life to the force that enkindles the human fraternity from the univocal essence of souls.

The Solar Opus

The *solar opus* begins when the changes that the "I" achieves in the astral body, through meditation, manage to impress themselves onto the etheric body, which is the body of memory, habits, temperament and instinctive sedimentation. Any inner change always ends up by becoming volatile and surrendering to the revival of ancient nature, if it is not impressed onto the etheric body. An instinct acquires power and invasiveness by means of the astral body, insofar as it has its roots in the etheric-physical.

Sedimentation and instinctive germination are continually nourished by sensorial impressions, to the extent that their subconscious movement conditions the content of mental picturing from the sentient sphere. In this way, the function of mental "picturing"—the activity that should mediate the autonomy of the "I" within consciousness—becomes continually inverted. The possibility of inner acquisitions impressing themselves onto the etheric body belongs to the "I," capable of moving within the soul according to the Logos, which is intimate and original to it.

As a principle, transcendent and nevertheless immanent to the "I," the force-Logos gives the "I" the power to impress the astral body's acquisitions onto the etheric body. It can be said that we, as pupils, attain the apex of clear consciousness, when we manage to intuit, within the force-Logos, something more than the "I" and nevertheless present within the "I"—a limitless power, but inconceivable to the "I" as its own production. We can talk about an essence of the "I," which is capable of overcoming the "I," and of acting through it as the Logos: all the more, the more the free "I" can be itself. The "I" supposes the Logos, but in supposing it, it receives the thinking that springs from its identity with the Logos.

Certain impressions, particularly erotic ones, invade the subtle zone of the etheric body to which suprasensory intuition, or the pure power of inner transformation corresponds by way of the soul. They paralyze each possibility to perceive and identify with the Logos. The imaginative *Eros'* continual process corrupts such a zone. This imaginative *Eros* is the opposite of creative imagination and, thus, the opposite of the "I"-being's central or "solar" impulse. The slightest subconscious erotic impression, that is, the most innocent impression, which for a man, for example, is to admire feminine features, and for a woman to be delighted in being watched with desire or to receive, in this regard, the compliments of someone who is not the one that has dedicated his very life to her, traumatizes that subtle zone, which is also the vehicle of pure intuition and of the Grail's virtue, or of the experience of sacred love. Rare are beings that can watch or be watched without being subjected to subconscious contamination. They know the independence that the "I"—insofar as it is identical to the inner Logos—possesses with respect to the astral body.

When speaking about the Threshold experience, it must be pointed out that the biggest barrier to it is the inner zone accustomed to agree constitutionally with the impulses of an obstructive Entity inserted in each individual as a "double"—one with which each individual identifies from birth. This "ahrimanic double" has indeed the task of furnishing us with the sensory perception of the world, but at the same time, it functions, by means of the nervous system, to impress the sensory—as the only dimension of reality—onto the soul. It is the zone of the sensual euphoria of corporeal physicality and of personal magnetism, but also of the subtle nourishment of desire, aversion, and fear—the sphere in which the will is mobilized for non-existent ends from the spirit's point of view and which, nevertheless, constitutes the incentive of human experience.

The freeing of thought is the initial mental independence from the zone of such an ahrimanic double, normally indistinguishable, because of its perfect inherence to neuro-psychic life—in typical forms of analysis that today assume the legitimate appearance of the unconscious. Profound concentration is always obstructed by the power adverse to inner freedom, which ascends from that zone. This power habitually uses the mental sphere. Therefore, in the mental sphere, the first liberating action occurs, but a patient elaboration of the processes of an ahrimanic nature also begins—processes turned toward possessing the initial, subtle forces that have been acquired.

To go beyond the Threshold is to free the profound etheric and impress upon it the golden stamp to which the soul has opened the passage by means of spiritual practice. According to alchemical symbolism, the *solar opus* is actualized as *aurea operatio Lunae*, to the extent that the Logos, which gives the "I" profound power, is the solar principle, the bearer of the Philosopher's Gold that penetrates the lower astral, or the "lunar body." In fact, by means of the lunar body, the ahrimanic double normally controls the life of the soul.

The golden liberating light has, as a vehicle, feeling that is elevated to the devotion of love, or "michaelic" *bhakti*, where what is the ideal of Rosicrucian spiritual practice is lit up. Such transfiguring devotion is possible, to the extent that it springs from the rigorous discipline of thinking, namely, from a spiritual practice of thinking and of the will, which ritually persists according to the rhythmic power of the center of the breath, right down to the purification of the ether in the depths. The required spiritual practice is concentration led to its maximum intensity and, simultaneously, to the absolute non-inherence to the etheric-physical body, from which springs liberated feeling—the true mystical force, capable of having a bearing on the etheric depths.

This influence is a subtle lifting of the etheric body from the bottlenecks of the physical organization, according to a creative musical power that is lost—a bestowing of autonomy upon the capacity of the etheric to stand up to the powers of physical minerality and, therefore, to transmit the soul's pure impulses—the condition of true devotion. Before this, devotion cannot be but a formative exercise of the soul.

The technique of this transformative influence is the *observation (animadversio)* of the limitless autonomy possible to the "I" by virtue of the Logos within it. It is loyalty to the path of thinking, namely, to the knowledge immune from dialectics, which does not allow itself to be deceived by the mirages of earthly powers (even if they are "spiritualistic"), nor by ready mysticism, of which the soul's dependence on corporeal nature nourishes itself. One must truly love devotion, in order to make of it a vehicle toward its suprasensory form, rather than a bond in accordance with sentient necessity. There exists an ecstatic and fervid tenderness, the art of which can be taught to us by the cat, or bear, or serpent. But it has always to do with the astral movement bound to physical nature—a movement that is not to be eliminated, but purified. It opposes the spirit, if it is not lived independently from nature, according to the light proper to the pure idea. Human love can reach as far as the physical senses, if it moves from its source as a free inner act.

The Higher "I"

The ultimate sense of disciplines, inner action and everyday struggles is to awaken the "I." In present-day humanity, the spirit appears as the individual "I." Within this "I," which expresses itself as the *ego*, is the Higher "I," the spirit, *Atma-Purusha*.

Although the spirit's whole power is present within the nucleus of the *ego*, normal egoic consciousness—with respect to the higher states of consciousness—is at a level of dream; with regards to other aspects, it is at a level of deep sleep. We are not truly awake in the waking state, but descend into the state of dream and of sleep each time we ascend to the levels in which we should realize our true state of wakefulness.

Disciplines, action and inner struggles are operations of the "I," but according to the limit of its precarious waking state opposed to the higher levels of consciousness, with respect to which, the "I" is in a state of sleep: therefore, according to a contradiction of its force, which impedes its real action, precisely in order to arouse it.

The non-corporeality of the meditative operation and its a-psychic-ness (which are to be brought to the highest metaphysical tenor) are technically fundamental. One must prevent the current of the "I," barely aroused, from becoming grasped by the psychophysical nature, as happens in all yogic-type operations and with deliberate pathological-ness in mediumistic practices. It should not be forgotten that the yogic-mediumistic impression is inevitable to each inner practice that ignores the conscious path to which we are referring, that is, the path of the "I"-being's real state of wakefulness, which can be experienced by liberating thinking, namely, the only activity of consciousness that bears as potential within its own movement, the independence from physicality. Normally, feeling and willing are perceived to the extent that they have already penetrated the physical organism. Only thinking can be perceived before it penetrates the physical, by means of the simple concentration on its normal movement.

In certain moments, each of us can be within the "I" or, rather, at the threshold of the "I." It is neither meditation, nor concentration, nor contemplation, but what in the end blossoms from them—namely, intuiting the "I" at a height independent of disciplines, and from this height, as what possesses the whole depth.

One then knows that the Higher "I" can operate only when human tension ceases, which in any case opposes it, even in the effort of concentration and of meditation. The emergence of the "I" is possible, when the world of foolish egoic ambitions quiets. The extinguishing of the *ego* demands the maximum power of the "I" within the *ego*. But it is not the *ego* that decides the emergence of the "I," even when it works toward its very extinguishing.

The Higher "I" works within the *ego*, according to an identity that the *ego* normally reduces to itself, by impeding the real action of the "I." Through the power of freedom, which descends from the Higher "I," but is actualized in individual consciousness, we can choose according to the ahrimanic or materialistic direction—opposite that of the Higher "I." But precisely because of this, we can freely choose the path of the Higher "I," or the Principle-Logos. The individual element and the Principle-Logos must coincide.

That which is truly the Higher "I," as a cosmic entity, or Principle-Logos, brought to humanity by the Christ, is so different from the "I"—as well as transcendent and inconceivable—that the "I," which bears this Higher "I" within itself, constitutes its greatest opposition, by identifying with its own individual earthly support. The "I" discovers the Christ force within it, seeing this force beyond its own support, as what is not it itself—which is before and after, and beyond the possibility of conceiving it. And with this, it absolutely actualizes its own individual being—the radical identity with the force.

At a given moment, one knows that the effort, the disciplines, and the rigor of spiritual practice are means of the *ego* still incapable of realizing its own extinction—an extinction that opens the passage to the Higher "I." This is present in the permanent "I," and in the *ego* that opposes it and, therefore, forces itself to survive by means of concentration, by means of meditation, by means of spiritual practice. The *ego* must expend all lofty ambitions, in order

The Higher "I"

for this loftiness to be realized as its death, its resurrection. Its everyday crucifixion has no meaning, if it does not know death and resurrection.

Through discipline, the *ego* prolongs its life and, therefore, its involuntary crucifixion, by resisting its own death and resurrection. The crucifixion must become an act of will, so that it can give rise to death and resurrection.

In reality, the *ego* tries to survive by means of spiritual practice, because it does not yet have the strength to get out of the way. It fears halting the effort to survive. It wants to keep the ultimate act to which it truly tends by means of spiritual practice from being fulfilled. The proceeding of the *ego* that meditates, concentrates, and attempts the paths of the suprasensory is its eager proceeding in time, because of its incapacity to stop itself, so that the power from outside the process of time can burst within the human being. This bursting of the Superhuman within the human crushes all the schemes of the *ego*, which therefore is inwardly led to delay it through the continuity of disciplines, undoubtedly useful to its force, but to the force that continually deviates and not to the authentic force capable of overturning the direction to which it becomes subjected: which is to say, capable of the individual direction of the "I," which initially moves by means of the *ego's* direction—a direction opposed to the "I."

There is a moment in which the arrest of all spiritual ambitions is the rising up of the spiritual. The "I"-being's self-removal—its disappearance—is its real birth. Its non-being is its being. The acme of the individual is the absolute affirmation of self-negation. Egoism, nevertheless, wills itself, even by way of its own destruction. It is a matter of understanding that it does not go destroyed, but only led to its non-being, namely, to its true individual being.

Meditating should continually end with a feeling of gratitude and a uniting of the soul with the Higher "I," namely, with the Logos. Moreover, what should be controlled are the impulses of the sentient and rational soul, which tend to make the final content of the spiritual practice their own. Only the Christ force within the soul can provide a way of keeping this content intact.

The Power of the Cross

Individual willful determination and its self-consecration, as positively opposite polarities, constitute the equilibrium of forces that continually intersect in the thoracic zone, otherwise called the "rhythmic center," or the "median center." The synthesis of forces can be perceived where the axis of light that descends along the dorsal spine intersects with the horizontal current, typically gathered at the height of the shoulder blades. The intersection point of these two forces corresponds to that for which Siegfried, unaware of it, was vulnerable.

It can be said that our Higher "I" is potentially present in this intersection of forces. We have the power to realize it. It is the intersection that is present at each point of the organism in which equilibrium is reestablished, or a cure begins, namely, where a lunar soul current comes across the corresponding solar current. Wherever the encounter of the two currents of force is realized, the Higher "I" lives, the Solar Human assumes control over the human being.

The image of this cross, evoked by us, is the first realization of the harmony of forces within us that corresponds to it. We feel it affirm itself along the back and operate as a liberating relaxation. When all is said and done, all disciplines converge toward this crucial harmony, which is actualized typically at the point indicated between the two shoulder blades, but realized in every other zone, wherever the vertical current of the "I" encounters the soul's astral forces. The non-encounter, or opposition, is human illness; the encounter is its cure.

To contemplate the back is to perceive the cross. The true force of the human being begins when the shoulders relax and the back corresponds to its liberating function in the median center: to the extent that it receives the virtue of the axis of light that encounters the soul's astral forces. Maximum calm, power, and the spontaneous donation of oneself arise from the median center, when the back becomes the bearer of redemption, according to the crucial schema. It is the schema of the most powerful life forces, which descend into us when, through spiritual practice, or through the confrontation of trials, a type of pre-agonic state is produced in us. By such a path, the Higher "I" of transparent will and of courage, assumes the reins of the human being.

The power of human redemption, which the axis of light mediates, springs from the cosmic correlation proper to the rhythmic center (thorax). Such a correlation is unconsciously contradicted by the mental sphere, bound to cerebralism, which creates, out of the axis of force, the vehicle of the *ego*—the obstructer of the rhythmic equilibrium, a producer of breakdowns of the psyche and the body. Along the spinal axis, the *ego* rules, according to the "I"-being's inferior sense, as the spirit of aversion. The profound opposition to the spirit, tenacious even in the most diligent pupil, runs as an illegitimate current along the path of light of the dorsal spine, creating out of it the path of what degrades and kills the human being. The legitimate current of the light of life flows when we confront the forces of death, the already mentioned pre-agonic state, by means of an intense inner life and the elimination of fallacious human supports. The "I" then receives the force-Logos, which lies within it, but to which it is usually closed and opposed unconsciously.

Freeing the mental sphere by way of the immediacy of the "I" consciously realized in thought, and by virtue of disciplines brought to proper intensity to the confrontation of the pre-agonic state, opens the way to the current of light that descends along the spinal axis. The light descends into the vehicle of willing capable of best overcoming the human, which, therefore, resolves the pre-agonic condition in sublime freedom. Its encounter with the Rhythmic Center is the experience of the Cross. Such an experience loosens the breath of our corporeal nature, to the extent that it actualizes a movement opposite to that of *pranayama*, which binds the breath to this corporeal nature, according to a technique legitimate to ancient humanity.

The peace established in the dorsal area on the basis of the crucial schema, after the moment of intensity and courage, must be contemplated, rather than physically felt. It is a pure inner state that demands to be received beyond the sensation of wellbeing that it inevitably entails. In effect, it must control the body from outside the body. Corporeality must not be introduced into the experience. The less it participates, the more it is permeated by the light, which is originally its own. In reality, the *ego* establishes its force on the sensation of itself. It lives off of the feeling of itself, which, within feeling, continually eliminates the spirit. This feeling, bound to physical corporeality, normally conditions the life of the soul.

In the crucial experience, feeling, freed of bodily nature, discovers its supra-individual connection. It becomes perceived as the life of the light. This life of the light does not demand the physical breath; it demands only the metaphysical movement of the breath (see "Respiration"), whose technique is advisable as the very secret of alchemy's final attainment—the Philosopher's Stone. The profound calm of the median center becomes the place in which the intersection of the solar current and the lunar current restores the lost, original human-cosmic equilibrium, which leaves animal breathing to itself, in order to actualize another type of breathing—that of the life of the light. It is the secret breathing that is absolutely incorporeal. It is the beginning of each resurrection, which, simultaneously, is the healing of the human being and the communion with the Divine—one process being inseparable from the other.

The most profound human pain is invariably the demand for the crucial rhythm's restitution, according to the essential need of the "I," which, not received as such by consciousness, brings about the disagreement of forces. The disagreement is constitutional to the *ego*. It is endured insofar as it opposes the restitution that is essentially demanded. The constitutional disagreement has ordinary breathing as its support. The crucial experience demands absolute independence from such breathing; the *yogic* breathing techniques, instead, reinforce it. The crucial condition, from which the new breathing can spring, is placed in relation to what in another paragraph is called "Astral Ataraxia."

In the case of difficult situations, or trials of a difficult moment, where the succession of attacks to the inner rhythm is more intense, the art is to allow the power of endurance—proper to the dorsal area—to act. Therein, the astral ataraxia opens the passage to the axis of the dorsal spine's light and, therefore, to the equilibrium of the Cross. In reality, the return of the force is the art of bearing the Cross. As pupils, we accept the trial and bear it as the path to the experience of the light's solar axis and of its intersection with the lunar current. Such an intersection is the beginning of the androgynous synthesis, which corresponds to the soul's primordial structure.

In the beginning, we gather the energies by not opposing the obstructive force. In this way, we loosen the tension in the shoulders and the back and make out of them, the force's place, to the extent that in this zone of the median or rhythmic center, as has been said, the vertical solar current and the horizontal lunar current tend to meet according to the power of the Logos. The more we allow the crucial currents of the "rhythmic center" to act through the wisdom of the back, by means of immobility and profound giving, the more we receive the healing virtue, and become the bearer of calm and the guardian of the crucial peace necessary to the Earth's inner state.

The encounter of the Logos' axial force with the soul's profound life is the power of the Cross that can be actualized when the soul overcomes its consonance with animal nature, which impedes it from realizing its own original nature. This original nature is a "stellar" structure, the confluence of cosmic forces, which the soul inwardly bears as a synthesis, by virtue of the unifying force of the "I," or of the Logos, but contradicts, to the extent that it becomes dualized, by identifying with corporeality. Through such identification, the soul knows only the mineral appearance of nature and of the Cosmos, namely, materiality. It cannot catch sight of its own cosmic structure.

The Logos-soul encounter is the principle of the reconstitution of edenic nature, which the soul bears within its non-conscious self—as the secret androgynous structure—by ordinarily making a destructive duality of it, by identifying with nature, from the mental sphere to sex. The Hindu Tradition's oppositional duality Shiva-Shakti that rules over creation, from which the transmuting circulation is normally impeded by the unifying current of *kundalini*—in whose form Shabda-Brahman expresses itself—is overcome in modern human beings by the soul's crucial union with the Logos.

The marriage Shiva-Shakti that, according to that Tradition, realizes the transformation of sexual power into spiritual power, capable of recreating human nature, is essentially realized by the soul, which, through the liberation of thinking and the corresponding purification, unites itself with the Logos, or with the essential force of the "I." Such a union reawakens the original androgynous power in the soul.

In reality, what gradually operates as the transformation of the dual current in the sexual sphere (see "The force of Eros") is prepared in the median center, according to the virtue of the Cross. Aroused by this virtue, it ascends from the lower centers of *Eros*, in order to reconnect with the forgotten source—the center of the heart.

The Force of Eros

The force of Eros is the primordial power of the spirit, devoid of its unifying virtue, or virtue of synthesis of the solar-lunar cosmic currents, of which it is archetypically at the origin, according to the symbology of Androgyny or of the marriage Shiva-Shakti (Logos and creative Power of Sound).

The essence of the force is within the heart. But there is an etheric center of the heart, and more internally an astral center and, still more essentially, a spiritual center, thanks to which the Higher "I"—one with the cosmic

"I"—is present within the heart. Within the heart, we bear the forces of the universe unambiguously gathered, and, at center of these (forces), the principle that rules over them. But, as an ordinary "I," we are outside such a world of powers. We ignore the secret of our own interiority.

There is no concentration in the heart by means of which we can minimally approach the world of powers within the heart. It is already an exceptional achievement for us to arrive at the perception of the etheric heart, inasmuch as we manage, by means of living thinking, to move within the etheric current, which, freeing itself from cerebralism, reunites the head with the heart.

Normally, we are cut off from this etheric current in the head, by way of the thinking that binds itself to the cerebral organ. In order to become conscious and dialectical, thinking separates from its own etheric current and actualizes a consciousness supported by corporeal sensations rather than by the etheric organism. A concentration of such consciousness in the heart can also arouse extranormal or extra-sensory sensations insofar as they are subsensory, but it remains nevertheless an operation foreign to the heart's etheric control.

The pre-dialectical perception of thinking, attained through the strengthening of such thinking—thanks to the discipline of concentration and of meditation—gives us a way to experience the etheric current that ascends from the heart to the head as a primordial power of the life of the light. Such a current moves according to a direction continually opposed unconsciously by the current of dialectical thought. Each yogic type of concentration, to the extent that it is unaware of thought's etheric liberation in the head, opposes the etheric current that ascends from the heart, as a direction of the cosmic "I" or of the Logos, which bears the greatest spiritual power of the human being.

If such a current is perceived and left ascending, we receive from it the inspiring principle that demands a specific suprasensory action, whose symbol is the Grail. We have initial contact with the heart's astral-etheric current. But we can only gather the keys to such a power by freeing the mental sphere from the cerebral system, which for us is to escape the rule of the zone from which *Eros* moves, namely, from the profound center of sex. By means of the cerebral organ, *Eros* governs the astral body and, therefore, keeps the action of the real "I" away from individual consciousness.

As pupils, we can work with unhindered autonomy on the center of sex, within the vehicle of the imaginative-volitive current that is awakened by virtue of an accord with the heart's etheric current. Such an imaginative-volitive current that is harmonized with the heart—even if it is still incapable of identifying with its transcendent center—acquires the power to descend into the depths. In effect, it moves from the center inside the forehead, running a straight line toward the neck, which descends along the axis of the dorsal spine, uniting with another direction of its force, at the height of the solar plexus. Its action tends toward that resolution of *Eros*' center, which will later give us a means to unite with the spiritual essence of the heart.

At the point of the dorsal spine that corresponds to the solar plexus, we encounter a type of extra-corporeal breathing—the temporary vehicle of the imaginative-volitive movement—insofar as this breathing is rendered independent from thought. The current, initially transmitted by this breath, is the dynamic synthesis of the two liberated forces of thinking and of willing, which have nothing to do with the currents *ida* and *pingala* of occult tantric physiology, whose dynamic belongs to a human type that is constitutionally different from the modern human being. Shabda-Brahman indeed takes on the form of *Kundalini*, but its manifestation through the physical form, *sthula*, is conditioned by the subtle (or etheric) form, *suksma*, which the human being experiences by means freed thinking.

The stone *cintamani* is simultaneously the obstacle and the passage toward the magic solar power. It symbolizes the cerebral organ, namely, the center in which we can experience the Grail's real content, inasmuch as we recognize within it the occult center where Divine love and the forces of death meet. Within this center, the work of resurrecting the life of the light from minerality is continually being carried out by means of the radical forces of the consciousness soul. This is possible because of the sacrificial gift carried out on Golgotha and the Logos' victory over darkness. The resurrection, however, is potential to the human soul, insofar as it correlates to the act of its freedom, namely, to the use that it can make of the forces of Self-consciousness at the present time.

This Divine love—the conqueror of death—can rise up as human love, or sacred love, if the *opus* of the Grail is realized by means of the consciousness soul's actual forces, which are normally alienated in the dialectical process. Thanks to a transcendent and, therefore, absolutely impersonal form of this *opus*, directed by the incorporeal powers of spiritual-corporeal wisdom, the pure mineral essence of our everyday nourishment unites with the pure substance of sensory contents, in a regal zone of the cerebral organ that was left intact since the breakdown of the "fall." We do not know this zone; nor did the great Yogis of India ever know of it. Today, however, it can be known thanks to the presence of the Logos in Self-consciousness. A regenerating etheric current carries out the synthesis of the pure essences of the mineral world, unusually resurgent as the mineral world reintegrated by the spirit. It is a power that, from the mineral sphere, ceases to grasp the human soul by means of desire. It no longer operates as the power of death upon the soul, insofar as it is corporeally incarnated. A power of death, in fact, normally opens wide the passage to sacred love and creates a path of the spirit's betrayal out of each human love.

The life of the light's current that operates in the secret regal zone of the cerebral organ is connected to the noetic liberation of the breath. Thanks to such liberation, the lance ceases to injure Amfortas. In the center of the head, the spiritual practice of thinking creates, from the sacred

Lance, Parsifal's magical weapon that restores the virtue of the Grail to Amfortas. The path of sacred love passes by way of the liberation of thinking. Thanks to such liberation, the breath's current of light becomes independent of the breath's median center. Moreover, it leaves intact, in a state of metaphysical immobility, the psychophysical apparatus normally interested in the breath.

We learn how to proceed by way of non-breathing. Having the negative breath's current as a support, we follow the path that leads to the realization of the Philosopher's Stone. A new type of breath is given to us. The Masters of the Rosy Cross see to it that the secret of this breathing remains unknown to the person who, despite the development of occult faculties, is able to make irregular use of them.

We can try for years to overcome the limit of egoic breathing and insist in connecting negative breathing to the sphere of the magical will, without grazing the secret of the Philosopher's Stone in the slightest. It is a knowledge that does not depend on human wisdom but, rather, on the dignity that the Masters manage to confirm in the pupil.

However, at a given moment, the activation of the etheric current is decisive, moving from a point halfway up the dorsal spine to the level of the solar plexus. Descending, it passes through the sexual center, in order to reascend the abdomen, again flowing from the solar plexus to the dorsal spine. In relation to this etheric current, the pupil allows the current of the will, that courses through the limbs, to act according to pure autonomy—an autonomy that arouses the analogous magical-volitive current of sex, normally governed by original desire.

The willing that courses through the legs down to the soles of the feet, in its non-corporeality, can be cognized imaginatively as the bearer of a pure autonomy, capable of acting, through etheric induction, on the current of willing that in sex normally becomes desire—the most profound. If the analogy of the liberating autonomy with respect to this current can be inductively realized, it again becomes the dynamic-luminous flow of sex's liberation, the vehicle of a union, in which the power of reintegration reaches the point where we normally lose ourselves in a voluptuous swoon. The freeing of corporeality's essential currents is possible. By means of them, the highest Hierarchies of the Earth's Solar Order operate within the human being—an Order mediated by the Brotherhood of the Rosicrucian.

The operation is possible for us, to the degree in which we have been able to actualize, within that current, the synthesis of two types of forces—mental picturing and willing—ordinarily separated in consciousness, insofar as it is a dialectical consciousness. One expresses the feminine principle, the other the masculine principle. Their separation, which corresponds to a constitutional dissonance in the modern human being between the nervous system and circulatory system, gradually destined to manifest as universal neurosis, is what normally paralyzes the soul's androgynous virtue.

The spiritual practice of thinking leads to the original harmony of the forces of mental picturing and willing according to a secret connection between the light with the life of the light, whose ultimate sense is for the high Mystery of Androgyny to awaken from its millennial sleep. Such a reawakening is identifiable with the experience of the Grail, or of sacred love, which bears the force of the Logos, thanks to which the resurrection can become realized as the initial act of our conscious will.

This current-synthesis of the two principles, masculine and feminine, is the human primordial force that can be reconstituted in germ in the spiritual practice of thinking, when thinking, by freeing itself of its dialectical presumption, becomes one with the current of the will. That which has been separated for long periods, is reunited by virtue of an inner act, which harmonizes the head system with the metabolic system. Such an act is the "primal matter" of the work that must be prepared by us. We cannot resuscitate the androgynous element that sleeps in the depths of *Eros*, if we do not prepare the germ of the synthesis (which, on the mental plane depends only on us) as an encounter of the thinking forces with those of the will. It is a possibility proper to the modern human being, capable of a thinking independence from the psyche.

The androgynous virtue, reconstituted as the nucleus of living thinking, thanks to the currents of the binomial polarity of consciousness, operates, in a resurrecting manner, in the forgotten, primordial androgynous current. If this is reawakened, its power—truly harmonized by the spiritual world—turns to the secret of the heart's cosmic-magical forces. The preparation of such a possibility is already itself a liberating introduction, which allows a glimpse into the ultimate meaning of the work—inconceivable to dialectical consciousness.

The current of desire is all called upon to burst with its dominating tendency. At the point in which it bursts, the androgynous conscious current meets it and does not allow it to ascend. Rather, it grasps its force and continues it, making use of its mobility in order to reach the center of *Eros*. We must imaginatively prepare this schema long beforehand, until the phase in which absolute coldness in opposition to the ascending warmth of erotic desire—continually stirred by sensory impressions and by the corresponding imaginations—is possible to us. A lower part is knowingly open to such impressions, while a higher part is absolutely independent of them and, therefore, able to go and meet them.

Until we have acquired absolute mastery over erotic impressions and imaginations, extended particularly to the subconscious, we cannot have the real solar experience of thinking, nor can we move beyond the preliminary form of imaginative consciousness. The longest and most painstaking work is to transform the "imagining" by means of which *Eros* controls the mental sphere of the human being, through the subtle channels of the cerebral organ. As the light of life's movement, thinking is, in itself, independent of such an organ, but, as normal rational thought, it becomes conditioned by the rhythmic-metabolic cerebral processes by means of which a rapacious *Eros* ascends to the mental sphere.

With respect to the dominion of the psyche, we must cognize the a-psychic function of purely logical-rational thought, as a function that is cosmic in itself, and as such, realize it, by intensely willing such thought by means of the technique of inner determination—typical of the modern investigator. In this way, we can have, with the brain, a relation independent of its vital processes.

Pure thinking, as the initial movement of the original synthesis, actualizes independence from the imaginative impulses of *Eros*. It can, at this point, give rise to the real imaginative movement—the opposite of what ascends from *Eros*. It is this willful imaging that can operate within the depths, as the initial power of androgynous reintegration, capable of encountering the current of desire where it resides. As long as such a current is capable of invading the mental sphere, the *opus* of imaginative freedom is impossible. It can continually be attempted and even initiated, but it continually becomes annihilated by the erosive currents of *Eros*. The highest human power, inverted, continually annihilates itself. It expresses only a moment of autonomy no matter how deviated toward animality, in the fulfillment of the act necessary for generating another being. But in that moment of autonomy, we are mandatorily excluded, having with the force only the dual relation, of desire—the animal relation.

The androgynous synthesis, which begins as the life of solar thinking, is led to encounter the "imagining" that expresses the inverse synthesis, that is, the synthesis opposite the "I"—the opposition Shiva-Shakti of Tantrism—rendered operational by the obstructing powers that make use of a degraded power of the "I." Such power, in its pure state, is the initial life of the "I," capable of overcoming the opposition truly unknown to the ordinary consciousness of the "I."

In the preparation of the androgynous "imagining," it is not a matter of not feeling erotic impressions, but of encountering what they really are outside one's rapacious identification with them. The spiritual practitioner encounters them by means of the imaginative independent current, at the center in which they form according to the power of the opposing synthesis. As ordinary human beings, we never encounter them, because we do not have the use of independent (or pure) perception with respect to them. We undergo them, that is to say, we feel them, whenever we are already wrapped up in them. We cannot encounter such impressions, for we identify with them.

Rosicrucian experimenters, who know the art of pure perceiving, bear this perceiving toward them. They meet them with the imaginative current that, within itself, has resolved the dyad, that is to say, it has realized the "sacred marriage"—the Sun-Moon connection, Shiva-Shakti. It has overcome, within itself, the duality of which desire nourishes itself. With such androgynous power, they encounter the duality's most profound power that requires the maximum tenor of the original androgynous power. Here, the Shiva-Shakti accordance, realized in the consciousness soul, is the decisive synthesis of the most powerful opposition, because *Eros* draws from it the radical power of irresistibility.

The experimenter that knows how to bring, into the depths, the forces of *Eros*' redemption is assumed by the Rosicrucian Brotherhood to be among the candidates of the *aurea operatio Lunae*—which is the experience of the Grail. The experimenter resurrects in imaginations of the primordial androgynous force, the current that continually takes life away from us and enslaves us to the currents of desire and of death.

The paths of *Eros* are the paths of the spirit's betrayal, the most powerful barriers to the current of the "light of life," namely, to the real current of love, regardless of their form—from the sensual to the passionate and affective, or sentimental, nevertheless moved by the desire of another's animal appearance, and not by the encounter with the soul's solar secret. To love according to the secret of the soul's solar Logos is the art of reviving the edenic Archetype, which we have intended to call sacred love.

The paths of the fall and of the "betrayal" can become the paths of reascension and of reintegration, thanks to the *aurea operatio Lunae*. The Archetypal Human expresses itself in an infinite series of forms of soul life, by dualizing itself through the sexes, all the way to the individual form that physically bears the imprint of differentiation. However, the component of the initiatory couple—retracing the original form's path of differentiation and of forgetfulness—realizes fidelity because one discovers in the other the synthesis of all forms, all the way to the vision of the Archetype that perennially emanates them.

Sacred Love

It is the relation that is longed for and continually destroyed by the human couple—the relation that operates in those rare moments of reciprocal self-donation from the depths of the soul, as the restorative virtue of the original harmony, which one does not presume to have lost and to be on the verge of discovering.

Each couple, moved by an immediate affective impulse, obscurely bears the calling of such a restoration, and, nonetheless, continually betrays it because of an insufficient opening of consciousness to the original element from which that calling moves. This element tends to resurface as an impulse of its unconditional self-giving, whose eternal power each of the two notices only obscurely. Continually, the shortage of soul life creates a parody out of the self-donation. It leads it to the loss of the presupposed suprasensory realm, which at that point requires the spiritual practice of a ritual of perpetuity and of conscious consecration. Such a ritual cannot come from traditional disciplines, but only from the spiritual practice of the new times, or "Solar Spiritual Practice," which the pupil can also identify as the path of the Grail. As we have shown, traditional disciplines ignore the relationship between the "I" and thinking and between thinking and the cerebral organ, which characterizes the inner constitution of the modern human being. They consequently ignore the type of feeling experience that can spring from the liberation of thinking.

In the current experience of love, the human couple has the momentary possibility of consciously resurrecting the sacred, but rarely notices it. To the extent that this couple does not cognize the irregular subjection of feeling to the nervous system and of thinking to cerebralism, it ignores where one can perceive what has lit itself up for it—even if this is its real ideal. It lets the awakened fire die out, because it ignores the technique of its essential sacredness. The content of this, however, is the heritage of an accord derived from previous lives, which tends to continue. The two make use of it unaware of its transcendence. They do not know that it demands to be continued by means of the current forces of consciousness, present behind dialectical consciousness. They gradually lose the blessedness that led them to declare eternal love for one another, near the zone of memory and of vision. Through time, from desire to desire, delusion to delusion, they vainly seek in other experiences the surrogate of the original cognition fleetingly intuited.

The couple that knows sacred love is truly "bitten by the Dragon," because it becomes aware of the soul's ancient ailment, and of the sentient soul's limit. It is said, moreover, that the "bite of the Dragon does not heal." The wound of Amfortas cannot be healed, but the Lance reconsecrated by Parsifal will cure it. One must understand this symbology. The bite of the Dragon is ancient, because it proceeds the epoch of Self-Consciousness. In fact, this epoch will be born as a result of the Dragon's bite. The bite of the Dragon is truly born as unconscious profound pain, which the sudden appearance of love can again heal, because the gift of the Redeemer flows in it. As modern dialectical human beings, however, we cannot know this Mystery; better still, we oppose it. We can become conscious of it, only if we overcome within ourselves the dialectical limit that is rationalistic and traditionalistic. The path of the solar spiritual practice can lead us to the Threshold of the spiritual world, where the decisive test—esoterically called the "Trial of the three monsters"—awaits us.

The initiatory couple cognizes, as an intimate soul process, what esoteric literature calls "the bite of the Dragon." This couple discovers it to the extent that it syntonically follows the solar path and begins to understand the power of the ancient wound's healing. The mneme of sacred love then decisively confronts the trial of the electrifying element of *Eros*, upon which it can affirm the light's flashing element. It also confronts the trial of the mundane and of the "overly human." It knows the experience of *Eros* as a path of degradation, but at the same time of the force that is victorious over the bondage of desire.

"The bite of the Dragon does not heal." For the initiatory couple, there cannot be the sense of existing, without the conscious restoration of fidelity to the proposition of sacred love. Even when it is called to such a proposition, the soul can lose the initial "life of the light" and unconsciously proceed again according to the imprisonment of the ephemeral. It is an imprisonment that appears exterior, but of which, in reality, there is nothing but inner liberation—the conscious rekindling of the metaphysical Fire, the re-conquest of the Mystery of the highest power capable of descending as the healing virtue into the earthly realm.

The lofty Mystery of the "light of life" is the virtue of the original love that the will reawakens, beyond the imprisonment of ordinary consciousness—an imprisonment that is projected in a legitimate dependence on one's sphere of life, in the bonds of karma, in the compulsion of human correlations. It is the trial that appears as the legitimacy of the "conventional," opposite the metaphysical proposition of sacred love.

Sacred love is the victory over the ephemeral correlation, which holds most of the *Eros'* force, and, therefore, controls us above as below, making us idealize the desire that, in reality, ascends from animal nature. Such animal nature, however, is perverted by desire's control of the mental sphere. The impulse of sacred love is not *Eros*, but the power of the Logos, which, in the soul, makes its vehicle out of *Eros,* until it is able to articulate itself within animal nature in order to transmute it. Those who truly conquer *Eros* actualize the primordial will of the "I," or the solar will. They inevitably encounter sacred love. But this sacred love, if received before such a victory—nourished with spiritual practice and self-giving—leads to victory over *Eros*, which is to say to its transmutation.

The spiritual practitioner who conquers *Eros* is initiatorily a solar hero. One cannot conquer it, if not for a love higher and freer than that nevertheless bound to the animal "appearing" of the human form. The enlivening force of such love is the "light of life" sprung from the sacrifice of the Redeemer. The stages of this sacrifice are to be known as stirring visions of the love that frees the Logos within the soul.

The bite of the Dragon that does not heal is fatal, unless we awaken within us the force capable of overcoming *Eros*—namely, the *Eros* that normally slays human love, even when it rises up according to a redeeming syntony. We must cognize the ultimate sense of *Eros*, before perceiving its power. We must cognize the secret of the resurrection founded on Earth by the Redeemer.

There is no love that does not need to be experienced within the soul as a resurrection from death in order to become sacred and true. In this way, it can restore on Earth the healing accord, which it bears as a radical longing within itself, and normally betrays continually. This longing is the longing for the resurrection. However, for it to be realized it must become, within the soul, the love that defeats death, so that it can overcome *Eros* and recover from it the "life of the light," by means of whose altered force it enslaves the human being. It is the longing that allows the spiritual practitioner to conquer the Dragon by drawing the impetus of combat and of victory from the suffering of its bite. In each being that knows the vocation of the everlastingness and the sacredness of the correlation, this longing lights up beforehand, according to spontaneity. But in order for it to become the power of life by means of the radical act of will, it must go through the experience of death and of resurrection, to whose course the ritual of the Son of Man has opened the passage.

What the spiritual practitioner attains as the victor over death within the soul's depths is the secret of the highest power attainable as a restitution of the edenic correlation and of the power to heal original sin. The solar spiritual practice leads to such a possibility, that is to say, knowledge becomes the perception of transfiguring love, according to the original proposition of the correlation, which is directed to the other being, deemed "infinitely loved," but normally not known as the bearer of infinity's secret. Only this knowledge can make a reality out of the affirmation of one's self giving.

Karma

With this Sanskrit term, it is worth indicating, among other things, the transcendent law by means of which all that manifests in the present life as "destiny" can be explained by causes sown in a preceding life. The doctrine of reincarnation is therefore presupposed—a doctrine that we need not consider in this manual, whose proposition is the practice of disciplines that lead to the direct experience of the truths alluded to in spiritual doctrines. Rather, we are interested in characterizing the sense of karma's presence in our everyday lives.

All that occurs daily, until appearing as physical facts—that is, as events capable of taking place on the sensory stage—reveals a karmic origin. It is not causal, improvised, or unexpected. Even if it appears that way, it is not.

According to the doctrine of karma, the event that occurs to the point of being physically perceptible has already been prepared—sometimes, centuries ago. It comes from processes in the past and is, therefore, in itself, already completed. Within it, even recent elements naturally converge. However, it is prepared with the involvement of different spiritual components, according to a prior impulse, which is absolutely rigorous in its logic. What has already taken place, the "fact," as the ultimate result of such elements, is always necessity—karma.

With regards to the form of the "fact's" occurrence, the present spiritual forces, namely, the forces of inner freedom, or of the independence from karma, are decisive. The form can undergo modifications in a positive or even a transformative sense, or even in a pejorative sense, depending on the presence of the "I"being's autonomy, or lack thereof. But its essential content, however, belongs to a reality already created, which awaits the responsible individual.

As the key to everyday events, such a view brought to a meditative level can provide its content of wisdom. The event is not there to provoke personal pleasure or displeasure, exaltation or execration, preoccupation or optimism. These are truly *maya*. The sentient reaction always expresses one's ignorance of a latent content, which instead demands, from the soul, the activity of a higher perception, foreseen in its development. It can arrive at this activity, by training itself to assume the fact according to an inner movement, which is not its pleasure, nor its displeasure. Pleasure and displeasure must be transformed into organs of perception. We must understand what "destiny" really demands by means of given events—particularly those to which one is more sensitive.

The event, like a symbol, tends to speak to us, or to teach us something. It is the world of necessity that makes an appeal to freedom, that is, to the inner free act, to thinking capable of essentially identifying with the object. The event is what initially appears inescapable as a fact, insofar as it lacks action, or inner content. This inner content must spring from the contemplative relationship of the event—the force that allows it to evolve. No event exists whose ultimate meaning is not the demand of a conscious act, namely, the reading of it. One is before the symbology of a language that does not ask us for sentimental or instinctive reactions but, rather, cognition.

The development of such a predisposition does not extinguish the capacity of feeling, or of loving, or of understanding by means of compassion. On the contrary, it elevates it to its highest form. It is the power of action as an expression of abnegation, to the extent that the action does not spring from an egoic reaction, but from the fact's objective content.

Find what an unpleasant event asks the soul, and this event begins to consume itself. Karma is a book whose language reveals to the experimenter the secret of the personal form of existence. To be free of karma is to possess the teaching that it personally gives by means of everyday circumstances and events—especially, the unpleasant ones. These can be interpreted in the most diverse ways from a subjective point of view, right down to their rational and psychological codification. But such a point of view gathers nothing of reality and makes each of us a continual laughingstock of events, with which the only relation is that of reflected thought and sentient reactions—the most obtuse relation.

To be independent of karma means to move beyond the world of ancient law into the sphere of freedom. But this involves penetrating the behind-the-scenes activity of karma. To be free means to act not on the strength of past impulses but, rather, by virtue of overcoming the ironclad concatenation of cause and effect, which is to act through love, interrupting the interminable spiral of necessity, and therefore, of human hatred. For example: a person who today kills another person who had killed him in a previous life, has evidently not developed the sufficient forces of freedom and love that allow him to escape the law of metaphysical causality that demands getting even. In the next existence he, in turn, will be killed by the other, if, in the meantime, the free "I" within this other person has not sprung up, namely, the free "I" capable of overcoming karmic necessity and of giving him, therefore, a way to expiate, by way of the soul, his own guilt, so that he, himself, is led in turn to find the free being within himself. The world's struggles and wars will not cease, as long as the law of karma totally controls the person incapable of asserting him or herself with the inner principle of freedom and, therefore, incapable of overcoming the ironclad mechanism of an "eye for an eye, a tooth for a tooth."

Nothing escapes the ironclad law of karma. The blows of destiny, mournful facts, illnesses, collective sufferings, catastrophes that strike entire populations, have nothing random about them. They are events structured according to an inner correlation, of absolute "mathematical precision."

In effect, each of us, every day, pays the debt incurred in previous existences. The concrete sense of life is to extinguish one's own debt in order to realize freedom. The problem is that we fail to notice it and accuse others of situations that regard only ourselves. The problem is also that the non-recognition is utilized as an instrument of a struggle that presumes to heal the situations of certain communities, from the damage of others. If we ignore the law of karma and of the inner principle that overcomes it, it is impossible to not keep the responsibility of our own difficulties from falling back onto our fellow human beings. Only beings gifted with exceptional morality are capable of accusing themselves and not others. A series of abuses that culminate in tyranny—with all the earmarks of the sociality and dialectics of a peoples' redemption—is naturally a karmic debt that the abused are paying. But, also, the lack of knowledge regarding the law of karma renders the tyranny possible, making the debt inextinguishable, for the fact that this debt is reconfirmed by the accusation directed to those apparently responsible. The unjust draws strength from the ignorance of the just. Knowledge of the law of karma in the modern world has been obstructed not only by Materialism, but also by false spiritual currents. The ancient juridical-sacral world becomes political-sacral today. The ancient "system" founded on the law and not on freedom, illegitimately governs today's World, by assuming the appearances of a social evolution that, in reality, has the task of obstructing—in particular, by preventing knowledge of the karmic behind-the-scenes-activity of the social question.

If the liberating knowledge does not grant a way to extinguish the debt by means of the soul's radical changes and the birth of impulses of real fraternity, karma affirms itself with mathematical rigorousness. It is not punishment, but the "I"being's profound will to realize its higher nature, resolving the debts incurred by the lower nature. Thus, the discomfort endured by a community as a result of abstract political measures is, indeed, the elimination of a debt, but simultaneously the preparation of the debt of whoever is responsible for such discomfort. Analogously, difficulties provoked by a strike that is economically unjustified and that does damage to social classes which already sustain, with difficulty, their own hardships will have to be answered by whoever has minimally (even if not persuaded) contributed to the strike and, therefore, to the sufferings that result from it—even if such hardships and sufferings are themselves a normal karmic debt. Thus, there is no money illegitimately removed from the human community that does not have to be restored. There is no illicit profit, embezzlement, peculation etc., for which one does not have to answer—nor is there any oppression, abuse of power, moral or physical lynching, false judgment, lie, or denigration. Everything is inscribed in the book of the law that corresponds to a justice that no one escapes, unless one knows the new path of freedom and of love, which leads one to desire the elimination of one's own debt and to cooperate in the elimination of some else's.

Daily, the scenario of life enables us to witness the manifesting of karma, namely, the self-affirmation of a law, which, today, after a millennial pause should find, within the human being, a free knower, namely, a person in charge according to an independence from ancient necessity, which is to say, according to love. Each day, we see beings that, unconsciously moved by the ancient juridical spirit, presume to change the destiny of others by means of ideologies and outer measures. Whereas, it would be essential that, first and foremost, they know themselves and, therefore, their own karmic debt, in order to be able to help others become conscious of their own (debt) and of the everyday responsibility with respect to its content. Such responsibility does not change because one lacks consciousness of oneself. Thus, for example, the author of a book that denigrates and morally destroys someone, or that falsifies an historic content, is not the only one responsible. Also responsible are those who contribute to its edition, right down to its distributors. Likewise, a pornographic book prepares the debt of even those who innocently cooperate in its preparation. The regular deformation of facts for polemical motives, slanderous propaganda, instigations that lead to clashes of factions and to violence, processes un-attempted for ideological reasons, incriminations devoid of real grounds for blame but needed for specific strategies, and each attempt at autonomy of the juridical organism—like what is cultural and economic—weigh karmically on those who are morally responsible more than on those who, insofar as they are executors, bring them to fulfillment. Those who by way of a nihilistic spirit destroy things, or objects, that are the fruit of human sacrifice and labor, will return with a destiny obliging them to reconstruct piece by piece what they destroyed, even if the times will have changed and the payment of the debt will have to take on another form. Of the rest, the vast population of the physically and psychologically disabled, of paralytics, of those with encephalitis, of schizophrenics, and so on stands before us as a question addressed to something more far-reaching than the tautological explanations of science, or the obvious human compassion.

No human measure can spare the consequences of karma from whoever bears its impulses within the forces that support our psychophysical organism. Everything is written in the structure of the universal Order, which bears the forces of a justice from which no one—materialist or spiritualist—escapes until the day in which the "I" within us awakens as a free being, capable of deciding beyond karma, beyond natural necessity, namely, by way of love, and by virtue of self-sacrifice—which is the message of Christ. When those who have the topic of fraternity and of sociality close to their hearts, love it to the point of dedicating their lives to it, they will not be able to help but discover that the social question is inseparable from the question of karma, and that knowledge of the law of karma is the transformative force of a future society.

Fraternity and Sociality

For as much as the theme of fraternity and that of sociality today seem to coincide, they do not, in their identity, escape the law of reflected thought, which creates the inverse out of each inner content, on the dialectical plane.

We have seen how modern human thought—by becoming dialectical, insofar as it is reflected by the cerebral organ—becomes the mediator of the psyche bound to corporeality, if it fails to convert itself through the typical spiritual practice of its own movement, in accordance with the disciplines summarized in this present manual. In reflected dialectics, devoid of the original inner element, the reflection's spirit of opposition to the light is inevitably expressed, through the reflection's contingent identity with the cerebral support, in which the impulses of the lower psyche operate.

Typically, fraternity is the sign of the spirit's presence in us, but, for this reason, its dialectics can substantially express opposition to the original content. Today, throughout the whole world, the fraternal relationship for series of beings is decided not by autonomous consciousness, but by a transcendent power, which possesses its indispensable system of information and regulation; it is decided by the group spirit that unites them, that is to say, by the regulation of the church, party, or race that unifies them. In essence, the limits of a fraternal impulse are established by ideology. Meanwhile, only beyond those limits could such an impulse really operate in the world.

The fraternity of such incorporated, or persuaded or catechized, beings is decided on the strength of political information regarding those to whom they intend to direct it. They include, within the circle of fraternity, those with respect to whom the information is the one required, excluding others as adversaries. It is a truly conditioned fraternity that explains the hatred and the inexhaustible war of the world. Never does it occur to any of the informed to double-check information.

In effect, the fraternity that thinks it is established through the correlation of a group and its regulations can begin only, there, where these regulations are obsolete, that is to say, where one is capable of a free act, for which another person is recognized to be spiritually identical beyond the normative indications of divergence. Fraternity, as a relation limited to the group circle, is not true. It is inevitably fiction, even if unconscious. It begins to be true only when it can overcome the circle of the group soul, in order to reveal itself to beings that appear outside such a circle. Only outside of this circle does fraternity begin to be true. There is no merit in loving those with which one agrees. Nor can this agreement be authentic, by rising up in function of the aversion.

Those of us who believe in society as well as in a true relation beyond distinctions of race, of culture, of party, or of church, establish a fraternal relation on the strength of the movement of one's own consciousness. One draws on one's own inner responsibility, rather than on the regulations of the director of conscience, or of the group organism. The profound solidarity of the "group" cannot but be in function of the aversion. Fraternity begins to take shape, when it operates independently of the verdict of the informative dictionary of political ideas, for use by the group.

A community, or a group, whose fraternity is arrested within the limit of its corresponding ideology—outside of which it sees beings with whom understanding is impossible—still does not know the New Testament. Without knowing it, such a community, despite the semblances of a social calling, still lives within the rule of ancient anti-social impulses, because it lives within the rule of the law or of the Herd—only beyond which is the experience of fraternity possible.

The word "sociality" can be legitimately given to a concept that includes everyone, and that does not exclude a people, or a current, or a social class, or a race. Rather, it considers each person as necessary and irreplaceable. This discussion collapses, or becomes naïve, with regards to the sphere of politics and its strategies, which demand, from one moment to the next, the passage from agreement to disagreement and, vice-versa. Such a method, in fact, impedes sociality from governing politics. On the contrary, in the all the world, the opposite takes place today. Politics assumes sociality as a pretext, which is the rhetoric of those who presume to provide for human needs, ignoring the extra-sensory structure of the human being.

Those of us who do not know how to meet another as a human individuality and do not recognize, within that person, a being with which a relationship unconditioned by race, church, or party is possible to us, cannot be called free. Such people need a director of conscience—political or religious—just as animals in a herd need a shepherd. Such individuals, despite their modern appearance, still belong to the ancient soul group. They are unconsciously racist, because an identical spirit binds them as a group to others, according to the psyche that is bound to corporeal nature.

In the pre-Christian world, fraternity, like sociality, was only possible to the extent in which it conformed to law—not to freedom. Truth and justice—not freedom and love—were able to spring from a transcendent standardization. In the modern world, the subsistence of the pre-Christian spirit in the current standardization of the group soul—ideological and political—is the survival in every region upon Earth of dead spiritual impulses, which are really anti-social, despite being clothed in pacifism and sociality. The radically anti-social impulses of the present-day supporters of sociality are truly at the source of incurable social injustices, class struggles and the inability to extinguish war.

Social thought is not yet capable of being alive, beyond the abstract dialectics of its likely common settings. What begins to be truly social is the thinking that transforms the human being—namely, meditating. Only by freeing an idea's movement from ideology, can we actualize, within consciousness, freedom from the group soul (see

"Freedom") and, consequently, fraternity as an expression of the free spirit.

The lack of fraternity on behalf of those convinced of a sociality learned rather than thought, hinges on the inclination to move on the plane of ideologies rather than on a the plane of ideas. It is rare that current theorists of sociality would know how to distinguish an idea from ideology. They do not believe in the reality of the idea, which, as a live germ, is the principle of fraternity and of sociality. Rather, they accept its dialectical product, ideology, because this has already interpreted the world for them, sparing them the effort to think. They are unaware that nothing can come from ideology. On the contrary, it is the opposite of the idea, for it is a reflection devoid of life, endowed with the power of the formal plausibility of its arguments needed by the ego, which fears having to reckon with itself, and to penetrate arguments with ideas.

When one does not know how to identify the error on the plane of ideas, one is led to combat the error in physical people, to which a class is assigned, neither more nor less than what is assigned to a race. One combats a prefigured class; yet one is, in effect, unaware of practicing a subtle racism.

In the system of an organized fraternity, an adversary is considered in which the greatest of dangers is recognized—an adversary, therefore, that constitutes the most hated class, to which the causes of all previous ills can be traced. Even a name that rings magically like a *taboo*, according to the inferior power attributable to such causes, is applied. Often, however, on the practical plane, it so happens that they do not become adversaries because they really belong to such a class. Rather, they occur as belonging to such a class, so that they can thus be stricken as adversaries.

The lack of sociality prevents the theorists of fraternity from recognizing that—as we have been able to mention in other pages—the true Adversary is really born within each of us as an ahrimanic double. But it is precisely this "double," with which we are unconsciously identified, that continually induces us to see, outside ourselves, the adversary upon whom we legitimately unload our responsibilities, continually.

The spirit of the Inquisition, which, at one time, established what lay inside and what lay outside the Church's infallible truth, is today reincarnated in the dogmatism of an ideological sociality, which truly lacks the living movement of thinking, or the idea—namely, what directly has the power within the human soul itself to separate what is social from what is antisocial.

Indeed, the accusation normally directed to the "system," to "society," to "class," and so on would be valid only if it were directed to such anti-social thought, dogmatically social, and, despite its progressivism, backward, like each dialectical intuition, in which the spirit is powerless to recognize itself. The spirit's self-recognition in each form of its immediacy—because of an obligation to honesty as well as to the purity of intuiting—is precisely the sense of the *spiritual practice* indicated.

Spiritual Practice

In simple terms, if one wanted to express the meaning of the series of the inner preparatory operations of initiation, one could say, without the fear of being mistaken, that it is the achievement of a lofty morality. It is the essential content of the meditative discipline contemplated in these pages. We can venture to say that, toward such an ideal, morality must, above all, elevate itself to the level of *saintliness*. Naturally, it is not a question of the morality to which one conforms, like to the series of agreed upon norms of good conscience but, rather, to the morality produced by the inner free act, like a *quid* that the spirit creates, almost always in the form unforeseen by the established norms.

The tenor of saintliness for the candidate of Initiation is not an end but, rather, a means, necessary to self-consciousness and to freedom, that is, to the purification of the sentient body, *kama rupa*, or astral body. At the same time, self-consciousness indicates the tenor of saintliness and of its wisdom not to appear as such— not to be an attitude.

It is easy to be good by being weak. It is easy to be strong by being wicked. It is difficult and heroic to be free, so as to be good through an excess of strength. But this excess arises as the possession and dominion of the capacity to be wicked. In fact, human freedom is founded on experiencing and becoming conscious of evil nature. There are spiritualists who, in function of their goodness, commit the worst acts of cruelty. An inability to be strong with respect to being wicked renders them "good."

The force's surplus is essentially the love for one's neighbor—the most difficult attainment, in that, the love for one's neighbor is almost always a pretense, prior to self-consciousness and the purification of the astral body, even when such love is expressed in acts of unquestionable praiseworthiness. It is the recitation behind which broods the longing for the spirituality that is not really possessed. With respect to this, the techniques that despise moralism and that contemplate an affirmation beyond rules have, within certain limits, a reason to be. It is a path of instant freedom.

But instant freedom will itself be a deception, if it springs from impulses of the astral body—called the "body of desire" in occult literature—not completely known, which takes the place of the "I." It is one of the greatest traps of the pre-initiatory phase, which is inevitable as a test of the "I"-being's real initiative. Each choice that is not the choice of the "I" is not free, for it belongs to the astral, to which all the mystical and initiatory attitudes—from the Gnostic to the yogic—are possible. The question of spiritual practice is truly a question of searching for the "I."

The spirit lies within the "I" that is independent of the astral body. But the "I" can operate within the human being so long as it immerses itself into the astral body, so long as it identifies with the faculties of the astral body—namely, thinking, feeling, and willing. Such identification is the inevitable weakening of the "I," before it cognizes the identity with itself at that level. It is its subjection to the functions that the astral body, by means of thinking, feeling, and willing, assumes in relation to etheric-physical -corporeality, namely, in relation to animal nature—functions, which, from the human mental sphere, are led to degenerations impossible at the animal level. From this, they are led to the constitutionally contradictory and ambiguous state of the "I," which operates through the astral body according to an identification with it—an astral body that acts in its stead, and that the "I" relies upon as a determining vehicle. It is an unconscious identity with corporeal nature. For this reason, the "I" that is the center, is not at the center. It does not express the spirit from which it moves, but it becomes the expression of nature, of race, of temperament, of the sentient and rational soul, namely, of the astral body, governed by Entities adverse to us, which tend to possess us. But, in fact, to realize itself as the "I," at that level, demands, from it, the development of forces, which it would otherwise never let spring from itself.

Only freedom from the illicit identity with the astral body, can give the "I" a way to identify with its very self and to realize—by rectifying—the higher nature of the astral, namely, thinking before it is a reflection of the astral, as well as feeling and willing, before they are an expression of the astral involved in sense life—namely, thinking, feeling, and willing as force currents, which are original in themselves and, as such, cosmic.

Spiritual practice is the undertaking of the "I," not of the astral body. The world of instincts and of passions that overpower us and paralyze the element of immortality within us is the astral body that substitutes the "I," by operating with the authority of the "I." It is the continual inversion of that original hierarchy thanks to which the spirit nevertheless substantially governs Matter, beyond every appearance of *chaos*. This inversion appears as freedom and is, instead, the paralysis of the principle of perpetuity of the "I," which alone can arouse the astral body's secretly perennial essence—the true meaning of spiritual practice.

The power of the astral body, withdrawn from the "I," operates against the "I" disguised as the instinctive current. The deception of all the false rebellions, of all ambiguous redemptions, of all apparent revenges, of all simple struggles against authority, can be recognized as a revolt of the "body of desire," or astral body, against the "I."

The revolt, which can give rise to one's own system, is not a human doing. It is controlled occultly by Entities adverse to the human being. When the astral does not resound according to the "I," and nonetheless acts with the authority of the "I," by claiming for itself a freedom that belongs to the "I," it is then the destroyer of life. Existence is then organized according to abstract relations, devoid of soul, but overflowing with dialectic. Extraordinary forces of intelligence and of will, which the above-mentioned extra-human Entities furnish, nevertheless support such a process. They tend to possess the human being, in order to express themselves on a plane cosmically forbidden to them, but one in which they can assert themselves by means of the power of human freedom—used negatively by us, and taken away from us.

Pedagogy

The general exaltation of the astral that is adverse to the "I," which can also assume spiritual forms, is the greatest obstacle to our current evolution. It is the principle of the so-called Counter-Initiation. Today, on an ordinary human plane, it is readied above all by means of un pedagogy that arouses impulses of freedom in the astral body of small children before the age in which it surfaces in them according to the rhythm of an occult cosmic law—the principle of the "I"—for which alone an undertaking of freedom can exist. According to the meaning of such a law, we can understand the question of freedom of the "I," in contrast with the necessity of the astral body.

Spiritual Science, from which springs a pedagogy aimed at the generations of the "new times," teaches that, in the first seven years, the child, according to the rhythm of the mentioned transcendent law—immanent to the "I"—is organized as a purely physical being; in the second seven years, as an etheric being; and in the third seven, as an astral being. Toward the twenty-first year, the "I" that, from the beginning has operated as a metaphysical principle from outside the body during the three periods of development, inserts itself into the physical-etheric-astral organism. From that moment on, we can experience according to the freedom of the "I." Freedom lies in the "I"-being's possibility to express itself, without being conditioned by the threefold structure—astral-etheric-physical—of which it clothes itself, but has as an obedient instrument.

If, during the first three seven-year periods, the impulses of an autonomy that belongs only to the "I" have been inserted into the adolescent's soul, these impulses inevitably act from the astral body against the "I," leading it to identify with them prematurely, insofar as they are illicit instinctive impulses. At the end of the third seven-year period, with the sudden appearance of the "I," these impulses will fundamentally oppose it, arousing the feeling of oppression and constriction with respect to any authority that moves from the "I." Meanwhile, only from the "I" can real authority and responsibility arise.

A young person who has lacked the discipline of obedience and of devotion necessary to the astral body, lacks the possibility of obeying his or her own central being, the "I"—the bearer of responsibility and freedom. The path of neurosis, but, more probably, that of criminality is open to such a youth, to the extent that the astral body—illicitly excited by the impulses of freedom during the years of the three seven-year periods—clashes with the "I" and tends to substitute it.

The inner formation of children, and therefore, their capacity to grow strong and luminous, depends on the moral climate established for them by a familiar environment. In the earliest years, the child, whose "I" still moves from the spiritual world, in reality lives as if in a temple, immersed in its sacred environment, of which it nourishes itself and of which it would not want to be deprived. Parents could learn the meaning of sacredness by wisely contemplating the child's natural being. Instead, it is precisely they who contradict and destroy it, with their frivolity, even if it is intentionally affective. More often than not, the child's cry expresses the pain of feeling the angelic world—in which the child is naturally immersed—removed by the fatuity of grown-ups. The destitute inner condition of whoever approaches children immediately acts upon them in a negative way.

The child's true spiritual level corresponds to that of meditation. Parents, who truly love their children, should construct for them an inner cradle made of their harmony and, if not from a precise meditative thought, at least from a sense of conscious religiosity. The child's sacred element is what will be later actualized within him or her as the power of the will. At present, this original element is literally rendered chaotic and inoperative precisely by those who presume to love and educate the child.

A correct pedagogy, moving from knowledge of the inner behind-the-scenes-activity of the child's formation, sees to it that the child grows in a way that his or her soul-physical forces are prepared to gather the "I"—the being that is truly free—gradually. This is a discipline of obedience, of devotion and of admiration, directed to all that in the scenario of the created bears the imprint of the sublime, of the abnegated, of the heroic. In this way, the spontaneity of the child is cultivated, as a form of its potential freedom.

We can grasp the inner behind-the-scenes-activity of the issue of pedagogy, and of the erroneousness of freedom's cult of impulses in the child's soul, before this very soul is formed and ready to gather the "I," if we bear in mind that the above-mentioned Entities, adverse to the human being, can act by means of the astral body. They can do nothing to the "I." The acceptance of the "I" at the end of the third seven-year period, is prepared by a suprasensory disposition, active as spontaneity in the child. In the first seven-year period, children are led to repeat mechanically all that they gather from their environment. In the second seven-year period, repeating evolves in children and is transformed into imitating. In the third seven-year period, imitating becomes the tendency to model oneself according to a higher human ideal. As we can see, the child's development up to the age of twenty-one, asks to be a wise preparation for the acceptance of the "I." Such a preparation is compromised by pedagogies through which Entities, fearing the birth of the human being's spiritual "I," act. They know that, through such a birth, the subjection by means of which they enslave the human being ends. They prevent the birth of the "I" by operating prematurely on the astral body and arousing its movements, which the human being will later mistake for its own free impulses.

Discipline, devotion, and admiration of higher models of life, are the same forces that direct the soul-physical being of the adolescent to receive the principle of the forces that is the "I," in which the spirit manifests and is thus the true human force, namely, the fount of courage, of loyalty, of creative imagination, of daring, of the inexhaustible will, of balance.

This contribution of the "I" is compromised by the pedagogy that cultivates autonomy in children before the appropriate time, granting them the indiscriminate expression of impulses, therefore, even of those that, ascending from animal nature, immediately take the upper hand over others. It is the not-so-wise pedagogical wisdom of the current time, to which is due the increase of neuroses and of criminality in the world, and of the vast fauna of the spiritually ill adjusted, who are gifted only with energy for realizing all that in them appears as instinct. This pedagogy makes, out of a young person, an unhappy unstable being seeking to avoid life, namely, a being led to compensate for the lack of internal order by means of whatever remedy, from drugs to passively becoming the pawn of the profane power's strategies.

The Path of Initiation

Only the spirit, as a principle distinct from the soul, can express itself in us as freedom without contradicting the laws of the universe. To the objection that can come from certain esoteric systems that affirm the Initiate's superiority over the laws of the universe, we reply that we are able to overcome such laws not by breaking them, through our inability to conform to them, but, first and foremost, by cognizing them. Only by cognizing them can we realize their principle within us, by rising up to this principle from the awareness of our own internal structure. The infraction is always the hysterical affirmation of freedom, which karma firmly corrects, if the adequate discipline of consciousness fails to intervene.

When the spirit is governed by impulses of the astral body, and the "I" therefore undergoes the form of the *ego*, each expression of freedom is the non-awareness that governs us, and finds through us, the ideological and juridical alibis necessary for its own expression. For this reason, the false individual freedom of one person cannot but bump against the false freedom of another. Today, it is the normal situation of human beings who allow the least spiritually evolved power to oppress, by means of their state of preestablished rights.

Only when freedom is an expression of the spirit that dominates the astral, and therefore, does not need to break its laws (insofar as it possesses such laws, by moving from its own essence, namely, from its own law), does free action coincide with moral action—but not insofar as the spirit conforms to morality, since such morality is precisely the product of its freedom, and not of rules. Rules are necessary there, where the spirit's direct action is not yet possible.

Initiation is the restoration of the spirit's original state, despite its human incarnation. Normally it loses this state, identifying itself with the soul, by assuming it as the vehicle of the correlation with corporeal physicality. Corporeal physicality imprints the soul and the soul engages the "I."

There is a preparatory phase, which takes place as the restoration of the spirit's original relation with the soul, or with the astral body—a relation that has always been the problem of ascetic paths and of esoteric wisdoms, to the extent that Deities operate within the soul in a way that is adverse to our freedom, as individual beings. For this reason, in ancient times the procedure of Initiation demanded, from the disciple, the "I"being's absolute detachment from the individual element. The "I" and the higher astral were separated from corporeality and the lower astral, and immersed into the spiritual world, so that there they could acquire the power of imprinting the golden-solar element onto the etheric-physical body.

In the modern world, Initiation can overcome the ordinary human condition, to the extent in which the spiritual practice is performed not by means of paths that lead to ecstasy or to *Samadhi*, but by means of the waking state realized at the level of the "I," which is superior to that of the ordinary astral—a conquest equivalent to realizing the consciousness that lights up in sensory perception. It is the waking state intensified in such a way as to realize the presence of the "I" within the soul, according to a state devoid of meaning for the ancient ascetic. In the modern human being, in fact, it is not the corporeal structure that binds the soul, but the soul, which through desire, binds itself to that structure, because of the scant awareness of its own spiritual nature at that level—a level to which, by now, it can arrive, as a spiritual element, only to the extent of being individual consciousness.

The waking state that is brought to fulfillment is that to which we have come by means of rational self-consciousness, by experiencing the individual "I" at the physical level, as was not possible for ancient humanity. Normally, thinking reaches its maximum intensity by expressing itself in sensory perception. Outside of this, it lacks intensity. Outside the perceptive support, it becomes weak, abstract. The task of spiritual practice is to actualize conscious thinking with the same intensity as when it is inserted into the sensory support.

Corporeality in itself has a chaste structure, which renders it capable of a direct relation with the spirit, of which we, immersed in the astral, are unaware. This chastity can be known in sensory perception; it is possible as an absolutely objective process, insofar as it is the spirit's direct relation with the corporeality of the sense organs. Instincts and passions that normally influence human judgment, by altering its objectivity, have no power over the objective function of the sense organs.

The fact that we, deprived of the suprasensory, perceive only the sensory realm by means of the sense organs, depends on the structure of such organs, modified though time so as to carry always less the suprasensory element that is inseparable from the sensory form, until we begin to identify content with such form. However, we have been able to attain the possibility of freedom precisely to the degree that it has been able to take on appearance as a reality. Only reality—not appearance—can, in fact, compel thought. Thought, which has only the numerical and logical appearance of reality, is potentially free. It is conditioned by the measurability of reality. Yet, by means of this measurability, it has the illusion of totally controlling reality.

Nonetheless, despite becoming the form of the sensory, the movement of perceiving is acknowledged as suprasensory in itself. As such, it goes nevertheless unnoticed, because for now consciousness lights up at the level of "appearing." The sense organs were so constituted that the suprasensory element would not disturb our physical vision—a vision necessary, in its exclusiveness, to the period of our egoic individual autonomous experience, For, inside of this, we could successively discover the suprasensory by inner means.

As modern researchers of the suprasensory world, we must be able to explain to ourselves exactly how the sensory experience leads to what we are seeking. Perception, in its pure objectivity, independent of psychic influences, is the spirit's direct relation with corporeality—a relation, which, as such, nevertheless takes place at a level of consciousness that corresponds to profound sleep. One of the fundamental techniques of solar spiritual practice, as we have seen (see "Pure Perception"), is lift into consciousness, by means of contemplation, the "I"-being's extraconscious relationship with the sensory realm in perception. The contemplative experience of the sensory process, by means of the perception of given entities with a physical nature, is one of the operations directed precisely toward the purification of the astral body, that is, toward the astral body's relation with the "I"—a preparatory relation of Initiation—and which has been pointed out as the conquest of the essential morality, namely, a therapeutics of the soul and the body.

Pure perceiving is an inner experience possible only to modern human beings. It was unknown to ancient (or traditional) ascetics, whose sensorial "perceiving" constitutionally bore its own inner content. The inner content was congenial to sensory perception. The modern spiritual practitioner must acquire it by means of the will. *Pratyahara,* as a Yoga technique, was a discipline meant to free the inner correlative activity from the sense organs, so as to utilize it for suprasensory experience. Meanwhile, pure perceiving, possible to the spiritual practitioner of today, is a "seizing" of the correlation in perception itself, with the aim of directly experiencing the metaphysical forces that the "I" expresses, by means of the sense organs, in physical reality.

The corruption of the sensory fact does not concern sensory perception but, rather, the use made of it by the astral body as the "body of desire. To the degree in which thinking inheres to the sensory content, such content manifests to us in altered form. Nor can we, as experimenters, grasp the direct relation of the "I" with the sensory realm. The perceptive content is always altered by the sentient soul and by the thinking that is inherent to it. Therefore, in the thinking with which we ordinarily think—considering ourselves autonomous—we are essentially controlled by impulses of physical nature and, therefore, passively guided forward by karma. In that sense, we, not being free, undergo our own karma. We are unable to know it as the force that has the power of operating right down to the physical.

Spiritual practice consists in freeing thinking from the content of the senses. Thinking, thus freed, reveals a content that belongs to it as an essence normally ignored, because it is never brought to manifestation. Such a higher essence is experienced as the primordial current of the uncorrupted astral and, therefore, as the source of the same astral body's purification. Going beyond in the spiritual practice, a transcendent event is possible. In such a current, the spiritual practitioner can encounter the presence of the Logos. The spiritual practitioner of today can find the Logos that ancient spiritual practices sought via the paths of ecstasy and of *samadhi*, Yoga and the specific technique of *pranayama*, within the intimate life of thinking—the intimate life, which in its pure form manifests as the power of absolute autonomy with respect to the lower aspects of the astral, or of the ordinary psyche. It is not yet the Logos, but its Threshold. It is up to us to cross the Threshold.

The type of thinking to which the experience of the Logos is possible, is the rational one proper to modern human beings, as an activity extraneous to the psyche—namely, abstract thought formed in the unilateral, quantitative, logical-mathematical experience of the sensory. It is the thinking of the "fall," the thinking of science, which, binding itself to the senses, must (as we have said) ignore the world's suprasensory content, in order to free itself of ancient spiritual authority, by knowing the world as quantity. However, freed of the senses, thanks to the self-movement possible to it at that level, such thinking can discover within itself, as an autonomous essence, the primordial suprasensory realm that has been lost.

The impurity of the astral body—normally the bearer of corruption, that is, of the original force's alteration—is healed by the presence of this original force in the innermost lymph of thought. The force expresses itself as the capacity to form rational concepts, which is the capacity of modern-day humanity, not of ancient human beings, who perceived the universals as living entities outside themselves. Today, we nevertheless use concepts without cognizing the force continually put to use for their formation. The spiritual practice is for us to experience this force. As we can see, it has to do with forces of knowledge. Regarding this knowledge, it was said that it becomes the power of morality, insofar as it is the bearer of the astral body's original purity.

Sense experience can become the direct experience of the spirit, insofar as freed thinking lifts the astral body to its real level. Hand in hand with the liberation of thinking, the disciple, by way of a specific technique, has a means to gradually experience, in sensory perception, the direct relation of the "I" to the physical world. This relation is, in itself, an act of absolute "transcendence within immanence," that we, as perceivers, experience and of which, nevertheless, we are unconscious. It is the act by means of which the "I" encounters at the physical level the suprasensory life of matter, or of the principle that rules matter—the suprasensory life never noticed as such in sensory perceiving. In this perceiving, we have the possibility of encountering the threshold of the spiritual world. We have the key to the forces that flow from the suprasensory realm into creative nature, simultaneously being compelled to deviate—by way of soul processes—beyond their support of physical life, toward the sentient sphere, thereby becoming instinctive powers.

In pure perceiving, as in pure thinking, we hold the key to the spiritual practice of feeling and willing, which can be experienced as original soul forces. Such a spiritual practice is called solar, because the inner force of thinking, of feeling, and of willing, flows from the Solar Logos, or from the spiritual principle of the Sun, which is the essence of the "I," but at the same time, the suprasensory essence of the Earth. The inner structure of the universe has at its center, the Solar Logos, and this is present as essence within the "I."

Initiation of the present era presupposes the spiritual practice of thinking, because within thinking, the consciousness of the "I" and of its correlation with the sensory realm lights up. As we have seen, the force of the "I," in its pure and therefore non-conscious state, is present in sensorial perception, as the spirit's initial identity with the physical world. Disciplines must give a way to experience within sensorial perception the same force by means of which the modern rationalist forms concepts, obscurely tending to reconstruct the solar nucleus of thought on the mental plane.

The content of Initiation is immutable, but its form demands a meditative preparation that corresponds to the current conditions of the pupil's consciousness. For the present age, preparation, as we have been able to observe, is essentially the spiritual practice of pure thinking, namely, of the very function for which thinking is called upon to operate in the exercise of concentration and of meditation. Such thinking, in its pure form, is the prerequisite of the disciplines.

Spiritual Healing

Spiritual healing is a service that we as spiritual practitioners can, if allowed, render to our fellow human beings, by mediating given conditions of their karma, thanks to an intuitive connection with the forces that express themselves within it. Therefore, the healing of illness is possible only if it is requested for others, not for oneself. One's personal wellbeing must be the result of the correct spiritual practice.

Solar spiritual practice heals the spiritual practitioner of illness, daily. Therefore, one does not subordinate it to personal therapeutic ends. Ailments should not be healed by such subordination. On the other hand, there are ailments that, sometimes, spiritual practitioners bring with them as aids, which, at a given level, allow them to not experience a truce with the animal desire of life; or as aids for the healing of another person's ills.

As pupils, we can be therapists not because we propose it, but because we cultivate the solar spiritual practice and, therefore, sometimes become mediators of another person's karma. We mediate the changing variations, in function of what is free of karma and, therefore, bears the metaphysical force of the Logos.

We become spiritual healers to the extent that we each do not presume to be one. Rather, we carefully hide the mediating faculty, by always attributing the merit of a cure to others. In reality, there is no such merit. Spiritual practitioners can propitiate the cure, to the extent that they operate as mendicants of the transcendent intervention that governs karma. We can be healers, to the extent that the world does not know it. Any role of healer attributable to us paralyzes our strength. Any cliché of healer with which we identify, hinders our lucid karmic relation—our mediating function.

The healer who is not a spiritual practitioner capable of connecting with the power that governs karma, and whose logic escapes all earthly logic, is not a true healer but rather a corporeal bearer of forces that are capable of expressing themselves etherically and of acting mechanically on patients, momentarily relieving their ills. These healers are useful to a certain limit and to the degree in which they conform to a rigorous ethic and to a style of absolute impersonality—a truly rare case. Nevertheless, however, their intervention is but temporarily useful. And they are themselves confined to a series of tensions, if not pretenses, of their force, when this force—to the extent that it is bound to physical corporeality—does not function, or becomes lacking as the body ages. Meanwhile, true spiritual practitioners have the opportunity of freeing the mediating forces more deeply.

Spiritual practitioners can be therapists to the extent that they do not presume to be so, and make sure not to appear as such. Their method consists, first and foremost, of leading patients to examine their lives morally, so that they can comprehend what, within them, must radically change, and thus take on a commitment with themselves. They lead patients to make an appeal to the necessary forces of the "I," to arouse and nourish such forces, so that these patients can begin to be self-healers.

When it is a question of true and proper illnesses, namely, organic illnesses, the cure can occur only if there is a decisive change in karma—a change that is granted by the spiritual world, provided that the extraordinary change occurs in the patient's astral body, such as the removal of inner causes. But, also, in that case, the essential requirement is the "I"-being's appeal to the innermost original force, namely, to the force that cannot be that of the ordinary "I." The fact that the principle of conversion, or of healing, or of renewing, is intimate to the "I" can be a major obstacle to this force, to the extent that the "I" identifies so much with its own human limits, as to not be able to conceive an inner force, beyond these limits. The secret of the Logos and, consequently, of each and every type of healing, is precisely in its being the principle that absolutely operates beyond such limits.

The healing practitioner can cooperate in the change required by the astral body of patients primarily by helping them become conscious of what they must change within themselves and, simultaneously, by means of profound prayer, which has the response of the spiritual principle, insofar as it is a request not for themselves, but for others. The power of prayer derives from the fact that it rises up from the soul of the spiritual practitioner, as the culmination of the greatest impersonality, connected to its consecration. It has to do with the infinite dimension of prayer, which indeed ensues from solar spiritual practice, but insofar as it is itself essentially harmonized by the spiritual principle.

A sick person can at times be cured in a prodigious way, but to the extent that the system of suprasensory forces allows it, thanks to the fact that a human mediator—a conscious spiritual practitioner, not a *medium*, but the opposite of a *medium*—operates as an intermediary of such forces. However, it is essential to bear in mind that it is not the virtue of healers or their capacity to use extrasensory forces that can realize a cure, when this does not reenter the sphere—even if ample—of karma's variations.

The intervention of a force of Grace, as mentioned, is possible in relation to what the patient knew how to let mature, even if only as an intuitive feeling of the human-supersensory state. This genuine sentiment, which is really an inner perception derived from suffering, can indeed be the open passage toward Grace. But from the moment in which this goes into action and the cure is realized, it is necessary, in order for its gift to be safeguarded intact through time, that the enkindling of that sentiment become a daily ritual—be it a living memory, that the soul can continually reattain, like an element of life that it needs no differently than the breath needs oxygen. The oblivion of the gift and the cessation of gratitude are a passage decisively reopened to the destructive forces that the reintegrating forces control, in an exceptional way, in the moment of danger.

The Function of Suffering

The function of suffering is to remove the soul continually from desire. Desire appears as pain so that it can again become the current of the "I," which the "I" needs to operate within the depths of the soul, right down to the etheric and to the physical. Pain takes form from any event that seems to elicit it. In essence, pain, demanded from the soul's spiritual depths, makes use of that event. We must not let ourselves be deceived by the thought that, if there were not that given event, pain would not appear.

Pain is what is demanded from the depths, when we are incapable of a profound movement according to consciousness, or spiritual practice, which is to say, when spiritual practice is weakened and becomes form, *routine*, or a habit devoid of inner life.

When suffering ceases, the soul normally does not have any other relation to the world, except desire. This desire readies further pain, unless one pursues the spiritual practice capable of transforming the power of desire into the power of the "I." For spiritual practitioners, suffering nonetheless continues alongside the provision of knowledge, in accordance with a relationship that changed with its function. Those who exhaust their individual debt deserve to accept that of someone else.

The obsessive permanence of suffering is essentially a power of the "I," deviated. The spiritual practitioner can assume it, without changing mediation, by referring the content to the "I," right down to its sensory expression.

When desire, which normally controls us right down to the physical, is removed only from the astral, and consequently remains as an impulse in the etheric-physical, the preconditions are set for illness, namely, for neuropsychic illness, with the series of its gradations—and, if the impulse in such form is not exhausted, (such pre-conditions are set) for a true and proper illness.

In that sense, illness is the form of desire's removal in the organic depths, of which the "I" is incapable by means of spiritual practice or catharsis. It is the astral body's radical demand, to which the current of the "I," operating as the life of consciousness, only partially corresponds. For this reason, the "I" is led to operate directly according to its original relationship with the etheric-physical, within the sphere of karma. The "I" can remove the limits of this sphere when, under the impulse of illness, its forces are capable of a specific metaphysical action. This specific action can be carried out consciously. Thanks to spiritual practice, it can establish a communion with the Entities of the Hierarchies that support the events of the etheric-physical organism by means of karma.

The Hierarchies nonetheless mediate the action of the "I" on the physical body. In reality, we have no other direct power than that of thinking. This power of thinking is what can be received by the Hierarchies and transformed into human destiny.

Suffering is a continual unconscious cooperation of thinking with the workings of the Hierarchies. The cure for suffering is the conscious elevation of thinking to the level in which it autonomously cooperates with the Hierarchies. When, by means of disciplines, thinking actualizes its own pure imaginative movement, it realizes the possibilities proper to such a level.

Inner Crisis

In the gradual work of purification, dissolution, and recombination of the soul forces, the pupil can go through moments of tension, of struggle, or of depression, which are really indicative of inner tasks or trials; they are foreseen moments of experience.

If we do not remember the sense of such moments and do not draw from the central principle of the "I," whose enucleation indeed demands to be radically measured up against the forms of the "human being," the situation can become severe and, if it is not adequately controlled, pathological. Overcome by such a situation, we, as pupils, have in this, a warning that there is something in our method that is wrong. We must turn back and start anew from the beginning. Our wisdom is precisely the humility of starting again from the beginning; with this, we draw again from the true force, perhaps with an immediacy and purity, previously unknown to us.

In the moment of crisis, however, we can be active to the point of controlling the phenomenon and drawing further knowledge from it about ourselves—the supplement of force that we really need. Moments of difficulty are, for us, an ancient limit reappearing again—an identical limit that asks us to overcome it, since we have effectively decided to overcome it in the depths.

In the moment of crisis, the art is nevertheless not to resist. Thanks to a minimal act of consciousness, it is to leave the movement free to the soul's decomposed currents, so as to arrive at contemplating it. It is what we call inner *judo*. In this initiative, which appears as a renunciation of the struggle, but is only the search for an initial movement of autonomy, the "I" knows the moment that it goes through and, by means of this knowing, it begins to assume the reins of the process. The soul's tiny *chaos* is possible thanks to the illegitimate use—on the part of the obstructive Entities—of forces that belong to the soul and which the "I" has the task of recuperating. In not resisting, in not opposing itself, in wanting to contemplate, the soul begins to gather its own forces.

The soul forces receive their pure circuit from the presence of the "I." The "I" begins to be present, wherever it begins to operate autonomously. Initially, this is "contemplating." In contemplating, the "I" begins to be independent and, in the independence, it gathers around it the soul forces, namely, the thinking, feeling, and willing involved in the chaotic crisis. The "I" must begin to operate within the soul. But with this, it realizes its own cognitive immobility with respect to the chaotic mobility of the soul—which is not the soul.

We do not yet know the soul, for the "I" has yet to penetrate it in the waking state. There is a profound area of the soul, unknown to the "I," because it is occupied by obstructing Entities, whose activity within the soul, the soul mistakes for its own activity. The initial movement of the soul's liberation is suffering, but the obstructing Entities take possession even of this, by inserting aversion and fear into it.

In fact, the first positive movement of the "I" within the soul is the experience of its own impotence. This gives it a way to realize the "zero" that its needs in order to move by itself, *ex se*. Abandonment, non-resistance, knowing the state of impotence, leads the "I" to that foundation of itself from which it can move, or affirm the power of its own metaphysical immobility with respect to the soul's chaotic movements.

The movement of the "I" is that of feeling itself to be outside the soul's chaotic movements: to look at them as something external. In this "contemplating" flows the force of the "I" within the soul. This force becomes withdrawn from the chaotic currents. The force of the "I," as the power of its invulnerable and, therefore, non-deposable centrality, operates to the extent that we are capable of evoking it. To intensely remember that, within the "I," exists the power that absolutely cannot be deposed, is already a surfacing of the "I"-being's presence. The crisis usually takes the upper hand through the "I"-being's lack of memory.

The memory of the "I" actualizes the presence of a transcendent power, which, even if unseen, is the absolute master of the soul forces. It must remember that it is really the Subject of the movements—the experiencer, not the experienced, with respect to the soul's movements. At that moment, the soul lives again.

Technically, the task is to isolate itself as the "I," from the state of the soul, so as to have the soul, objective, before it. Non-resistance and letting the chaotic currents go, is essentially the first movement of the "I." Furthermore, the "I" immerses itself, or sinks into the soul's *chaos*, but its movement is indeed not that of "becoming lost" but, rather, a descending with its decisive force into the Will sphere, where, in reality, a struggle takes place. To abandon itself; to cede willfully; to immerse itself into an inner state, is essentially the "I" entering into depths of the soul with the reorganizing force. It is clear, however, that such a descent of the "I" must be prepared by means of a specific spiritual practice of the imagination and of the will.

The art is not to combat, in order to allow the "I" to combat. This is the secret of victory in each soul trial. Not to combat (undoubtedly similar to the Taoist non-action) is essentially the art of not allowing the involved soul to act; it is to forbid oneself from reacting with the soul's tension and weakness. It is a matter of working to connect the problem to the "I"—namely, the chaotic movements to the "I," the weaknesses to the "I," the soul to the "I." That is to say, it is to unload everything onto the "I," namely, onto the principle that can truly sustain everything. The more pain it sustains, the stronger it becomes, within the soul.

Here, one can comprehend the real meaning of painful trials. They are always a demand for the presence of the "I," namely, the stimulus by which we can observe carrying within ourselves the force that can do anything. Instead, we are obtusely led, as in ancient times, to lean upon the soul, by means of which at one time we were legitimately connected to Atman, or to the Tao, or to the Buddha.

The spiritual practitioner of today must attain the sagacity to travel the path of the "I." Traditional methods do not lead us to the "I," but to the soul and to the body. They bind us evermore to our psychosomatic nature, namely, to our weakness.

Only the "I" can descend into the soul and into the body and cognize the soul's convoluted forces, and experience them without being touched by them—rectifying them. This descending is essentially an ascending, a perceiving of the original forces. The essence of the "I" is the principle of invulnerability and of the absolute identity with the world's creative Entities—the principle that does not know contrasts, but only unambiguousness. The presence of the Logos in the "I," as its innermost essence, is not only the possibility of curing any type of breakdown of the soul forces, as well as the path to the reconciliation with things, with our fellow human beings, with the world, but, above all, it is the principle of the resurrection of what is original and cosmic within the structure of the soul, by way of trials, which in reality are brief moments of death.

Anguish

Anguish is the psychic resounding of an altered physical condition, nearly always a neurotic depression, which does not manage to become a true and proper illness. In that sense, it is to be therapeutically dealt with on the physical plane. Internally, we must remove the causes. Thus, we must first and foremost, identify them. From an occult point of view, one is in the presence of a "vampire" type of force that was able to reach the physical organism, from where it exercises its power on the etheric and on the astral.

For inner therapy, an image-key: anxiety as a pond into which the strongest current, which moves it and renders it fluent, must be allowed to enter. Anxiety must be employed as the vehicle of a more powerful flow to which a passage can be opened. Anxiety overcome is always the principle of a more resolute balance of the soul.

A technique: to discover within ourselves the psychophysical contraction that aims to be valid as a defense against anxiety, and to loosen it; to not resist anxiety, but to let it be until it reaches its maximum expression; to attain a sense of calm powerlessness with respect to it; to make use of it as a support, to which we let ourselves go, until realizing the sense of the uselessness of each opposing force, which, in reality is a part of it. The sense of powerlessness and uselessness is to be pushed to the extreme, until we give it our whole being, by allowing the whole force to coincide with it; to abandon ourselves to a state of annihilation—zero, the principle of calm, but simultaneously the state necessary to the Higher "I" so that it can assume the initiative and operate with its authority.

Zero is the willed annihilation of the desire of life. Anxiety, in fact, is nothing but the sign of the desire of life, disappointed, whose delusion becomes piercing, right down to the physical. We must tend toward "zero" as if it were to a pure nothing—a functional ataraxia—into which we can sink, like into an abyss, letting ourselves fall as if we were dead. We must die to what wants to be in such moments, despite ourselves—namely, the state of anxiety, which tends to annihilate us. We must utilize its force of annihilation, until it becomes a willed annihilation. We must lead this process to the utmost depth, all the way to the exhaustion of foolish ambition. Such an exhaustion of foolish ambition, if we observe, counts as an offering of ourselves to the spiritual principle. At this point, in fact, the "I" has a free path. It can take charge of eliminating the soul's obscurity and of establishing its force and its security.

The transformation of anxiety, by becoming meditation, leads to the thresholds of the "I." In reality, anxiety is a demand of the "I." It obscurely and tensively demands the awakening of the "I." It appears with the insistent fixity of a force of nature, to which one must oppose an equal power of conscious insistence, namely, that of profound concentration, which renders the action of the liberating force possible. Such concentration can directly use the power of the basal inertia (see "Inner Crisis"), which is the corporeal *facies* (appearance) of the deepest willing.

Tiredness

Tiredness is almost always illusory, regardless of its form. The rest that eliminates it is always an inner process, independent of corporeality and, in that sense, capable of radically operating upon it.

In the tiredness of muscular system, we have the opportunity for the physical organism's positive self-abandonment, which promotes the activity of thinking free of corporeality and, therefore, at the same time, corporeality's maximum rest. We can use the condition of physical tiredness as a vehicle of corporeal calm (which is essentially inner calm) because, in such a condition, the etheric body spontaneously tends to free itself of the consciousness bound to the physical organism. In essence, we have available the state of physical relaxation required by concentration and by meditation.

The only possible obstacle to the inner utilization of tiredness is the ready intervention of sleep—pursuant to an impulse in which we spontaneously give ourselves over to it—regained precisely by virtue of an inner predisposition. It is up to us to resist this intervention of sleep, or even to make use of it in order to free ourselves of tiredness. We must observe, however, that outside such a deliberate abandonment to rest, sleep is an obstacle to meditation. It is the means used by the lower nature to reaffirm itself, by annihilating the change produced by concentration and meditation. This event naturally has nothing to do with the demand of normal nightly rest.

Tiredness only regards the nervous system. The phenomenon is to be observed in light of the following principle, namely, only the physical brain really gets tired, not the etheric current (which by means of the brain manifests as thought), nor, therefore, the etheric body. The etheric current, from which thought arises beyond the dialectical threshold of consciousness, is by its nature inexhaustible. Actually, the more it is strengthened, the more it is led to offer its activity.

Thinking, independently of the cerebral organ, could think to infinity, thereby strengthening itself more and more. The physical instrument of thinking—the brain—gets tired, but not thinking. Precisely because thinking is bound to its own physical instrument and, therefore, to the impressions of the senses and to sentiments and to correlative impulses, its physical instrument gets tired; it deteriorates; it becomes the center of breakdowns of the psychic life, the origin of nervous illnesses, of depressions, of anxieties, and of the corresponding series of illnesses.

The true healer of tiredness, just as of every breakdown of the nervous system, is the thinking that realizes its autonomy from the nervous system and, therefore, unites, in the etheric sphere, the soul with the "I." Thinking can give the etheric body a way to operate on the physical, like it does during sleep. In reality, during concentration, thinking that concentrates on a single point, produces in resting consciousness, a condition whereby the "I" and the astral body are freed from the etheric-physical, analogous to what happens during sleep. It is a condition of sleep near the maximum state of wakefulness, in which the edifying action of the "I" is possible.

Normally, thinking must unite with the life of the senses, in order to be awake and conscious. For it is not yet capable of the state of wakefulness and self-consciousness on the basis of its own extra-corporeal principle, that is, without sensory support, which is to say, without the mediation of the cerebral system. Such mediation binds the life of the soul to the nervous system more than is necessary. It is, therefore, not only at the origin of tiredness and of the various forms of onset of the emotional-instinctive life, but of all the physical illnesses.

The overcoming of tiredness, like that of every physical and psychic illness, always comes from a reestablished circulation of the "light of life"—that is, of the etheric body's *dynamis*. In that sense, we can comprehend what is thus the required technique, if we bear in mind that the dynamic sphere of thinking in its formative, or pre-dialectical, moment is precisely the etheric body. The formative force of thinking is the etheric force. Concentration and meditation, when they correspond to the peculiar canon of the present-day human being—a canon deemed "solar," insofar as it corresponds to the soul's relationship with the solar Logos—summon the etheric current whose metaphysical stream is the Sun, but whose essential center is the human heart—though certainly not the physical heart. One who possesses concentration and meditation can, by means of the solar canon, direct the etheric body's currents, so that they, thus, reunite one's "human" being with the principle that bears the Divine in the human (see "Rules of Initiation," etc.).

The Joy of Existing

The joy of existing is always a deception of the soul that desires corporeal life rather than its own life. True is the joy of being—what the soul knows when it experiences sensations as an incorporeal content within corporeal being. Such content has nothing to do with the corporeal instrument by means of which it manifests, since it is, in reality, the soul experience of the "I"—normally ignored.

Sensations are not deceitful. But what is deceitful is the soul's swooning in them. The joy of swooning is the pleasure of evading, or of sleeping, or of avoiding the struggle, of fleeing from responsibility, of eluding the inner discipline. The joy of swooning is communally accepted as the joy of existing. This joy regularly readies pain. It is deceitful, because it ignores its own real content, which is independent of the senses, namely, a content whose true function is to nourish the soul, not its dependence on the senses.

Rarely is joy pure. Nonetheless, it can continually be rendered pure if its resounding within the soul is identified as a non-sensory process in itself. Then, it becomes the nourishment of the soul and of life. Even the joy considered to be inner is bound to the senses, because modern human beings have a mental life founded on the nervous system and, therefore, unconscious of the metaphysical element of thought—the element that expresses itself dialectically by means of the cerebral nervous processes, even though it is, within itself, independent of them.

By normally depending upon the senses, joy is always the prerequisite of pain. It is not an error as sensation, but as a sensation that enslaves the soul. It inevitably readies pain, to the extent that it opens the soul to vibrations that are not in harmony with its essential nature. On the contrary, these vibrations oppose its essential nature. The pain needed by the soul to correct the ephemeral state of sensual joy—in which authentic joy, as a soul event, is excluded—always arouses events, which appear painful as outer facts. In reality, the "I" is excluded.

The joy of being and the joy of serving the Divine, or of expressing the Divine that is intimate to the soul, coincide. When joy is not identical to the joy of serving the Divine, it readies pain. The joy of existing, through the contradiction that it bears within itself, continuously readies pain, which the soul needs in order to discover the suprasensory content of which it is continually deprived in the sensory realm.

Physical joy, always sought, is never truly possessed. To possess it metaphysically is its ultimate sense. The longing for it is never satisfied, because the soul seeks its own content in a sensation that continually eliminates it. Therefore, it seeks it in further sensation, in which it again loses it. It is thus led to grasp it in forever-new sensations, by means of a desire that gradually strengthens itself.

As spiritual practitioners, we experience pure joy, because we train the soul to feel every pleasure, not as its own swooning, but as its own content, separable from the sensory form. In another area of the soul, we feel the blessing arise that previously seemed to us to arise from the senses. In reality, this blessing rises up by means of the senses, but it belongs to the more lofty soul, since it is united with the activity of lofty cosmic entities. For it is a movement of love, whose ultimate (or real) sense is solely that of being offered to the spiritual world. There is no joy of the physical world whose substantial aim is not this offer. Each joy that escapes this consecration is a theft perpetrated against the suprasensory world. Therefore, it occultly readies pain.

In reality, the soul's swooning in sensual joy excludes the area of the soul in which the "I" is present—namely, the soul's element that is, in itself, divine. It has nothing to do with forbidding oneself the normal joy of the senses and the spontaneous immersion in it, but of continually referring it—and this is possible in some cases even later—to the true experimenter, to the "I": through contemplation and penetration of the mental sphere, it gives rise to the "I." Within the "I" is the Divine.

Enjoyment, which is normally the path of the human being's animalization, can become the vehicle of the spirit—a magical vehicle. As spiritual practitioners, we train ourselves, with given sensations of joy, to extract from them the soul's pure movement—the *dynamis* of the light of life, in accordance with the real spagyria. We learn the art of separating the sensations' content of light from sensual swooning, which is the continual destruction of such content. For a similar technique, see the entry "Pure Perceiving."

Diet

Diet is not a decisive factor for spiritual progress. Nonetheless, at a certain phase of development, nourishment that is in keeping with the knowledge of the effects of substances on the subtle bodies has its importance.

A meat-based diet—because of this nourishment's type of constitution— leaves inactive within the pupil some deep assimilative astral-etheric forces, which are instead called upon to act when they find themselves in the presence of the plant element. For they have to elevate the substance of this element to the level of the animal's organization. Volitive forces, deeper still, are called upon to act opposite the mineral element—which is now essentially the case with medicinal substances. And so, *tea* blocks concentration, while coffee appeases it. Legumes bear an element of "tamasic" heaviness, because they lack the solar element capable of arousing the activity of the organism's solar etheric element. Meanwhile, grains nourish without bearing weight. Tubers, in general, and the potato in particular, demand a digestion that takes advantage of a specific activity of the central nervous system—to the detriment of the inner faculties that can be aroused thanks to an independence from such a system.

The spirit's real physical opponent in the (human) organism is alcohol. According to Rudolf Steiner,

> Our relationship with alcohol undergoes a transformation, when we become permeated, even etherically, with suprasensory knowledge. Alcohol, in fact, is still something absolutely unique in the kingdoms of Nature. Within the human organism, it reveals itself not only as the provoker of weight, but above all, directly as a force antagonistic to the inner impulse of the "I." If we observe the plant in general, we see how within its organization it normally develops a force up to a given point. An exception is the grapevine that takes it beyond such a point. What other plants reserve uniquely and only for the new germ, all of the vegetative force that is otherwise reserved only for the new germ and that does not overflow into the rest of the plant, this force, in a bunch of grapes, overflows in a determined way even in the fruit's pulp, so that, by means of so-called fermentation, by means of the transformation of what is formed in the grape and, within it, brought to the greatest tension, there is created something that effectively has a force, comparable only to what our "I" has on the blood. What is, therefore, developed as alcohol from the juice of the grape, is something that is created in another sphere of Nature, since it is similar to what we must create when, from our "I," we exert an action on the blood."

Rudolf Steiner continues:

> We know the inner relationship that the "I" has with the blood. It can be characterized outwardly just by the fact that when the "I" feels shame, blush rises to our face. Meanwhile, when fear or fright is felt in the "I," we become pale. This action of the "I" upon the blood—no matter how present in it—is, in an occult sense, totally analogous to what occurs when the process of the plant is led to unfold backward, in such a way that what exists, for example, in the pulp of the grape, or that generally comes from vegetality, is transformed into alcohol. The "I," as we have said, must normally create in the blood a process—occultly, but not chemically speaking—totally analogous to what is provoked when, so to speak, one traces, backward, the organizational process of the grape's pulp, by drawing out of it a chemical product—alcohol. It follows that, by means of alcohol, one introduces into the organism something that acts upon it just as the "I" acts upon the blood. One therefore receives, by means of alcohol, an antagonistic "I," in direct opposition to the action of the spiritual "I." In reality, an internal war is unleashed, or, in the final analysis, one condemns to impotence all that emanates from the "I," when alcohol stands opposite it as an antagonist. This is the occult condition of things. Whoever does not drink alcohol is insured the full possibility of acting upon the blood by means of the "I." Whoever drinks alcohol, does exactly as one who would like to demolish a wall and, while pushing from one side, simultaneously positions someone else to push from the other. In this precise way, with alcohol use, the activity of the "I" on the blood is eliminated. Therefore, whoever nourishes one's life with Spiritual Science, feels the action of alcohol on the blood as a fight directed against the "I," and knows that true spiritual evolution encounters a

grave impediment, if it procures for itself this opposition" (*The Effects of Spiritual Development*).

Furthermore, with respect to the same theme, Steiner expresses the following:

> Alcohol is to be absolutely avoided. The vegetarian diet is not indispensable, but favorable. (*Guidance in Esoteric Training*)

> Naturally, when one wants to develop the astral body, the most important operations are meditation and concentration. Avoiding alcohol in all its forms is particularly important; even those sweets full of alcohol have a damaging effect. Alcohol and spiritual exercises lead to a dangerous terrain. (*The Temperaments*, 1904)

Again:

> Rudolf Steiner was asked one day what influence could alcohol have on a pupil following a specific occult path. He responded, "To this question there is no answer: in fact, if one is an occult pupil, he or she cannot drink alcohol" (L. Kleeberg, *Wege und Worte*)

> An associate once asked Rudolf Steiner what inner consequences should a member of the "esoteric class" who drinks alcohol, expect. The answer was: "In that case, he or she is not a member of the class" (W. Simonis, "German Bulleton," n 67)

> Whoever wants to understand the doctrine of reincarnation and be lifted above one's transitory personality, must abstain from drinking alcohol. Whoever drinks wine, will never attain the vision of what is impersonal to the human being" (Mar. 17, 1905).

There were ages in human history when wine was unknown. In the time of the Vedas, it was virtually unknown. In the ages when there was no drinking of alcohol, the idea of previous existences and of many lives was universal; no one doubted its truth. As soon as human beings began to drink wine, however, knowledge of reincarnation rapidly faded, eventually to disappear entirely from human consciousness. It existed only among the initiates who took no alcohol. Alcohol has a peculiarly potent effect on the human organism, especially on the ether body, the seat of memory. Alcohol obscures the intimate depths of memory. "Wine induces forgetfulness," as the saying goes. The forgetfulness is not only superficial or momentary, but also deep and permanent, and there is a deadening of the power of memory in the ether body. That is why, little by little, people lost their instinctive knowledge of reincarnation when they began to drink wine. (*An Esoteric Cosmology,* pp. 33–34).

Rules of Initiation

Discussed are the rules of initiation given by Rudolf Steiner to pupils of the Esoteric School, in the year 1912 (Italian translation edited by the author).

Here, the conditions at the heart of the current day initiatory preparation will next be described. It is impossible to realize improvements in that direction, by means of provisions pertaining to outer or inner life, without the fulfillment of such conditions. All meditations, concentrations and other exercises become devoid of value, and even dangerous in certain regards, if life is not ordered according to the conditions mentioned. It is not a matter of giving us forces. We can only develop those that already exist within us. They do not develop on their own, because outer and inner impediments obstruct them. The outer impediments are eliminated by means of the following rules of life. The inner ones are eliminated by means of particular indications that regard meditation and concentration.

I

The first condition consists in attaining thinking that is perfectly clear. To that end, we must, even for a brief period each day, at least five minutes (the more, the better), become free of the disordered fatuous lighting up of thoughts. We must become masters of our own world of thinking. We are not masters, if outer situations—any profession or tradition, social relations, belonging to a given people, or the demands of particular moments of the day, the need of disengaging from a given task, etc.—involve the need for a type of thinking and the means of carrying it out. In that brief period of time, we must, therefore, by way of free will, completely empty the soul of the everyday run of thoughts and, out of our own initiative, place a single thought at its center. We must not believe that this has to be a lofty and interesting thought. What we must achieve in an inner sense is even better obtained if, from the start, we force ourselves to choose the least interesting theme possible. In that way, the autonomous force of thinking is stimulated to the greatest extent, and this is what matters. Meanwhile, an interesting theme is, itself, what drags thinking with it. It is better that this task of controlling thought be undertaken with the theme of "pin," rather than with that of "Napoleon the Great."

We each say to ourselves, "I move from this thought and, by means of pure inner initiative, I associate with it all that can be appropriately connected to it." At the end of the exercise, thinking must remain before the soul as bright and alive as it was in the beginning. One practices this exercise day after day, at least for a month. Each day, we can propose for ourselves a new thought. We can however keep the same thought even for a number of days. At the end of the exercise (2nd phase), we try to bring to full awareness the feeling of inner steadfastness and security, which, with more subtle attention, we will quickly notice within our own soul. We concentrate it at a point just inside the forehead, between the eyebrows. We conclude (3rd phase) by imagining a line that moves directly from this point toward the neck and that descends along the median groove of the back (from the brain to the spinal column), as if we wanted to reverse that feeling in that part of the body.

2

When we have exercised in this way for a month, we add a further requirement. We attempt to impose an action upon ourselves that we would certainly not complete during the usual course of life. We then transform this action into a daily obligation. It would be good, therefore, to choose an action that can be accomplished daily for an extended period of time. And it is better yet, if we begin with an insignificant action, to which, so to speak, we must obligate ourselves. For example, we set ourselves to water, everyday, at a fixed time, a plant, which we have acquired for that very purpose. After a while, a second action must be added to the first, then a third action and so on, until one can do it without hindering other daily duties.

This exercise must similarly last at least a month. But, inasmuch as possible, we must even during this second month, continue the first exercise—even if we do not take it up as an exclusive duty, as we did during the first month. We should not give it up; otherwise, we will soon notice how the fruits of the first month go lost, and how the usual flow of uncontrolled thoughts begin anew. We must be careful that results, once attained, do not go lost. When we sufficiently possess such a completed action through our own initiative by means of the second exercise, with subtle attention we become conscious, within the soul, of the awakened inner impulse (2nd phase). Therefore, we again pour out such a feeling, so to speak, into our own body, so that it can flow from the head to the heart (3rd phase).

3

During the third month, the exercise of equanimity must be placed at the center of life; we must train the soul to be even-handed with regards to the oscillations of pleasure and suffering, joy and pain. "To lift the cries of jubilation to the Heavens and to be afflicted unto death," must be consciously substituted by a stable disposition of soul. We must take care that no joy runs away with us, that no pain depresses us, that no experience moves us to anger or to unbounded worry, that no wait fills us with anxiety or with fear, and that no situation alters our normal equilibrium, etc.

We should not fear that such an exercise makes us dry or apathetic. Instead, we will notice that in place of what is lost by means of such an exercise, luminous soul qualities arise and, thanks to a subtle attention, we will be able one day to notice an inner quiet within the body (2nd phase). As in the two previous cases, we again pour out this sentiment similarly into the body, by allowing it to irradiate from the heart to the hands, then to the feet and lastly to the head (3rd phase). We must not demand such an operation after each single exercise, since, in effect, it has nothing to do with a single exercise but, rather, with a continuous attention directed to the life of the soul. At least once a day, we must recall this inner quiet before the soul and then undertake the exercise of allowing it to flow from the heart. With the exercises of the first and second months, we behave as we did with that of the first month during the second month.

4

During the fourth month, we must take up a new exercise, that of positivity. It consists in seeking out what is good, excellent, beautiful, etc. in all experiences, entities and things. This soul quality is efficaciously characterized by a Persian legend of Jesus Christ. While He traveled a road with His disciples, they saw, lying along the edge of the road, a dead dog rotting away. With repugnance, they all turned their eyes away from the sight. Only Christ stopped, thoughtfully considered the dog and said, "What wonderful teeth this dog had!" Whereas the others had seen only the repugnant, the unpleasant, He found the beautiful. Thus, we, as esoteric pupils, must aim at seeking the positive in each and every manifestation and each and every being. We will quickly observe that under the cover of what is repugnant—even beneath the features of a delinquent—something good is hidden; behind the appearance of a crazy person, the divine soul is nevertheless hidden.

This exercise is in some way connected with that called "abstention from criticism." One must not understand the matter as if one needs to call what is white black and what is black white. There is, however, a difference between a judgment that springs from a contingent personality and decides according to sympathy or antipathy, and the point of view whereby one places oneself, full of love, in an outer manifestation or in another being, by asking oneself in any case, "How does it come about that a person manages to be and act like this?" Such an attitude immediately offers to help what is imperfect, rather than confining itself to cursing or criticizing it. Here, the objection cannot be raised that the life conditions of many human beings demand that they curse and judge, given that these conditions prevent those concerned from a correct occult training. There truly exist life conditions that largely render such training impossible. The disciple should not really, despite this, impatiently expect to realize attainable improvements only in given conditions. If, for a month on end, we consciously orient ourselves in our experiences according to a positive vision, we will gradually observe (2nd phase) that a feeling surfaces in our inner being, as if our skin became permeable everywhere and as if our soul opened amply with respect to the subtle and occult processes of its environment, which before completely escaped our attention. It is truly a matter of combatting the lack of attention that exists in each of us with respect to such subtle things.

When we have observed that the described feeling manifests in the soul as a sort of blessing, we then try (3rd phase) to mentally direct this feeling toward the heart, in order to allow it to flow from there into the eyes and from the eyes into the space around us. We will notice that through the effect of this, one achieves an intimate relationship with space. We grow, so to speak, outside of ourselves. Furthermore, we learn to consider a part of our own environment as something that belongs to us. It is necessary to apply much concentration to this exercise and, above all, recognize that each tumultuous, passionate, element saturated with emotionalism, acts destructively on the spirit's cited disposition. As we repeat the exercises of the first months, we still keep to what has been indicated during the previous months.

5

During the fifth month, we attempt to cultivate, within ourselves, the feeling of confronting, without bias, any new experience. We must decisively get rid of that attitude for which, regarding a thing barely heard or seen, we ordinarily say to ourselves, "I have never heard this; I have never seen it; I don't believe it; it is an illusion." We must be ready at each moment to find ourselves before a new experience. What we have until now recognized as regular and ordinary, must not be a restriction for gathering a new truth. Even if expressed in radical form, it is absolutely just that if someone approaches us, and says, "you know, the tower of church X is completely leaning tonight," we should nevertheless leave the door open to such news, namely, to the possibility of believing that the knowledge that we have acquired of the natural laws can quickly be expanded thanks to such an apparently unheard of fact. During the fifth month, those who turn their attention to acquiring this disposition will note (2nd phase) a feeling that surfaces in the soul, as if in that space of which we have spoken regarding the exercise of the fourth month, something became alive, as if something within it awoke. This feeling is extraordinarily delicate and subtle. We must seek to attentively gather (3rd phase) this subtle vibration in the environment and allow it to flow, so to speak, through all five senses, namely, through the eyes, the ears, and the skin, insofar as this contains the sense of warmth.

At this level, we must not direct our inner attention to the impressions that flow through the lower senses, such as taste, smell and touch. It is not yet possible for us to discern the numerous negative influences mixed up with the good ones that exist at such a level. It is therefore to our advantage to put off the spiritual practice of these feelings to the next level.

At the conclusion of the five exercises, during the sixth month, we must finally try to systematically resume all of them by repeating them with regular alternation. Through the effect of this, a harmonic balance of the soul is gradually established. That is to say, we will notice how all the bitterness relative to the disagreement between the world's appearance and reality disappears. A conciliatory disposition toward all experiences takes possession of the soul. This is not indifference; on the contrary, it renders it capable of working toward the betterment of the world. A calm understanding begins for things that previously were completely indifferent to the soul. Even one's walk and gestures change under the influence of such exercises, and one day we, as pupils, will even be able to observe that our handwriting has taken on another character. We will consider ourselves to be near the first level of spiritual ascension.

As we have seen, the initiatory discipline is comprised of three periods. The first is the fundamental exercise, which works on the etheric body's connection to the physical body. The second is the contemplative attention directed to certain aspects of such a connection's resolution. The third is the orientation of the etheric currents that one thus arrives at determining: from the head to the dorsal spine; from the head, through the heart, into the body; from the heart to the whole person; from the heart, through the eyes, into the surrounding environment; from the enlivened environment, a movement of return toward our being.

The 3rd phase of the 3rd exercise can be valid as a synthesis, if, by way of its movements, we trace the pentagram, using an image of ourselves with arms horizontally open—which is to say, by way of a line that goes from the heart to the right arm, until reaching the hand, and returns, by turning below, to the left foot. It then goes back up high, in turn, to the point between the eyebrows, before again flowing below—with a similar straight line—to the right foot, and finally reascending toward the left arm all the way to the hand. From there, it goes back to the heart, in order to repeat the movement.

Yet, again, two recommendations must be emphasized. The first is that the five exercises paralyze the damaging influence provoked by other occult exercises, so that only what is beneficial, remains of them. The second is that, on their own, they properly ensure the positive outcome of the work of meditation and concentration. For the esotericist, not even the pure and simple, though conscientious, observance of the current morality suffices, for this morality can be subtly egoistical, if we, for example, operate with uprightness in order to appear upright, or to consider ourselves upright. The esotericist does not do good deeds in order to be considered good, or in order to consider him or herself good but, rather, because he or she knows that only the good enables evolution to progress from one level to next; while evil, stupidity and ugliness pose obstacles on the path to this evolution.

Bibliography and Further Reading

Romero, Lisa. *Developing the Self: Through the Inner Work Path in the Light of Anthroposophy.* Great Barrington, MA: SteinerBooks, 2015.

———. *The Inner Work Path: A Foundation for Meditative Practice in the Light of Anthroposophy.* Great Barrington, MA: SteinerBooks, 2014.

Steiner, Rudolf. *Anthroposophical Leading Thoughts: Anthroposophy as a Path of Knowledge: The Michael Mystery.* London: Rudolf Steiner Press, 1973.

———. *Anthroposophy in Everyday Life.* Hudson, NY: Anthroposophic Press, 1995 (includes "The Four Temperaments").

———. *The Effects of Esoteric Development.* Hudson, NY: Anthroposophic Press, 1997.

———. *An Esoteric Cosmology: Evolution, Christ, and Modern Spirituality.* Great Barrington, MA: SteinerBooks, 2008.

———. *Guidance in Esoteric Training: From the Esoteric School.* London: Rudolf Steiner Press, 2001.

———. *How to Know Higher Worlds: A Modern Path of Initiation.* Hudson, NY: Anthroposophic Press, 1994.

———. *Intuitive Thinking as a Spiritual Path: A Philosophy of Freedom.* Hudson, NY: Anthroposophic Press, 1995.

———. *An Outline of Esoteric Science.* Hudson, NY: Anthroposophic Press, 1997.

———. *Start Now! A Book of Soul and Spiritual Exercises.* Great Barrington, MA: SteinerBooks, 2002.

www.ingramcontent.com/pod-product-compliance
Lightning Source LLC
Chambersburg PA
CBHW031145160426
43193CB00008B/257